AF538906

Transforming the Dry Lands

The Sadguru Story of Westen India

Harnath Jagawat

foreword by
Prof. Yoginder Alagh

N M SADGURU
WATER AND DEVELOPMENT FOUNDATION
Post Box No. 71, DAHOD - 389 151, Gujarat, India

India Research Press
B-4/22, Safdarjung Enclave, New Delhi – 110 029.
Ph.: 24694610; Fax : 24618637
www.indiaresearchpress.com
e-mail : bahrisons@vsnl.com

2005

ISBN : 81-87943-58-0

Cataloging in Publication Data
Harnath Jagawat
Transforming the Dry Lands : The Sadguru Story of Western India
by Harnath Jagawat

1. Water / Management 2. Development
3. Biography 4. Dry Lands.
I. Title. II. Author

Printed in India at Focus Impressions, New Delhi – 110 003.

Transforming the Dry Lands : The Sadguru Story of Western India
by Harnath Jagawat

Contents

Preface

For the last about 30 years, I have been engaged in serving the cause of poor tribals in rural areas in three Indian States of Gujarat, Madhya Pradesh and Rajasthan. Being a student of rural development and the Founder Director of an NGO, N M Sadguru Water and Development Foundation, popularly known as Sadguru, which is known nationally and internationally for its expertise in the field of integrated water and land resources development, I had been thinking for a long time to find time and write about my work and experiences. Several of my friends and well wishers in academics and colleagues as well as funding organizations also encouraged me from time to time to write a book. But busy as I was with my institution building and other organizational responsibilities, I hardly had any time to spare for the purpose. But as they say there is an opportune time for every thing that one is destined to do. So at last that time arrived and so also an opportunity. For the last couple of years, I had been waiting for Dr. Katar Singh, an old friend and well wisher, to retire from his post of Director, Institute of Rural Management, Anand (IRMA), and to help Sadguru in improving the status of its training institute and the quality of its training programmes, besides providing guidance in documentation of Sadguru's work and experiences. That time also came and Dr. Katar Singh finally relinquished his office in August 2002. I reminded him of my long-standing demand on his time and he agreed to help. So the process of actualization of my dream to write a book got on the way and has culminated into this book.

The book is my modest attempt to document what now has come to be popularly known as the Sadguru Model of Rural Development. The Sadguru model has attracted the attention of several reputed scholars and national and International organizations engaged in rural development, including Indian Planning Commission, which has shown interest in its replication in other tribal areas and backward districts in India. This is just an example to illustrate the relevance of the model and the interest in its replication coming from the highest planning body of India. Outside India, some features of the model are being implemented in Ethiopia under a Triangular Co-operation Project among India, Ethiopia and Norway.

The goal of Sadguru NGO is to promote sustainable, equitable and eco-friendly socio-economic development of poor tribals in its project area. Sadguru has pioneered a new approach to tribal development. The approach uses water as a catalyst for development and focuses on community-based water resources development and management projects. Sadguru's work over the last 30 years or so has led to substantial improvement in the socio-economic conditions of thousands of poor households. Besides, Sadguru has been instrumental in creating many NGOs and building their capacity through training, and provision of technical and financial support. All those NGOs are also engaged in tribal development through judicious use and management of local land and water resources. Consequently, Sadguru directly through its own projects and indirectly through other NGOs has brought under the fold of micro watershed development nearly 300,000 hectares of the land. Sadguru itself has developed some 500 water resources development projects which are being managed by empowered village communities successfully.

Over the last 30 years or so, I have written large numbers of papers, notes and reports on various aspects of rural development and have attended several conferences and seminars on the subject in India and abroad as both a resource person as well as a participant. Whenever, I got some free time from my busy work schedule, I would write about my experiences, particularly, about the problems I encountered while doing my work and how those problems were resolved. Thus, over a time, I accumulated a lot of material pertaining to Sadguru's work and experience. I have drawn upon that material for writing this book.

The book has eight chapters, which together cover all important aspects of rural development, with the main focus on natural resource development and management. In this book, I have tried to combine my personal observations and experiences with the professional work done by me. The reader would get a feel of it through out all the chapters of the book. As Editor, Dr. Katar Singh has helped me in improving the articulation of my thoughts, ideas and experiences and putting them in academic perspective.

For motivating me and helping me in bringing out this book, I am indebted to so many people, to my many colleagues, the finding organizations, my friends and well-wishers and importantly, Dr. Katar Singh, who has ungrudgingly helped me writing, editing and bringing out the book in this shape.

Harnath Jagawat
Dahod., January 2005

Foreward

Success means to work competently. If we are innovative, we develop new ways of doing the work that we are trained for or involved in or at least we try to perform our duties fairly. Many people are not leaders, though success is usually thought of in those terms. Most of us lead a normal life. There is however, a different breed of women and men, who refuse to accept injustice or incompetence and excuses for not taking on the bigger issues that plague us. Such people are not normal in the day-to-day sense of the term. As the social psychologist, Eriksen points out, they question social values and try to change the existing order of affairs.

My friend Harnath Jagawat is one such person. He refuses to accept that the adivasi is destined to a life of poverty and ignorance. At a very young age, together with his wife, Sharmishtha, he decided that the water, which flows through the lands of tribals, can be harvested for their development and once it is available, it would produce the wealth with which they would prosper. It was an outrageous idea and most people felt that it would fail. Where would the energy come to take the water from the wells up the hills where the adivasi lives? Where would the resources come from? There were many other objections. Jagawat, however, persisted and succeeded. In this book at one level he discusses the technical aspect of the work and at the other level he discusses the larger facet of development. It is a useful book for the development practitioners, policy makers and students. The interest of the book however lies in another direction.

Jagawat like many of the women and men of his breed talks of his experiences. He talks of his village, his association and love for village. The women and men he worked with. The ones who gave him faith when the world looked bleak. Others who were always hostile. Many incompetent. His moments of despair and his hours of acclaim. It is this, which makes it a very interesting book. Jagawat is a practical man with the professional orientation and so writing is not his forte. But, for someone willing to bring in change, this is a very rewarding book.

Jagawat talks of the partnerships between the social sector and business, for which Gujarat is famous. In his own words: "Though the money provided was relatively small as compared to the budget, particularly in the last few years, it was crucial for the survival and growth of the organization. The managerial expenses for several years were met from the contribution made by the Mafatlals. This provided a great deal of security to the organization and paved a way for further progress through raising funds from various other sources. Both my wife and I were on the payroll of the Mafatlal Company and this arrangement continued up to the year 2000. This arrangement made me feel that whenever I was raising funds, I was not asking for my survival."

He feels that natural resource management is the only panacea for the tribals and their development and begins with the obstacles faced from the statuesque. (I relate an incident from the book: "In those days, nearly three decades ago, the role of NGOs in irrigation development was neither accepted nor encouraged. The technical department would say that irrigation was their field and that NGOs had no business to entering into the field. While the then Chief Engineer, Irrigation Department, was prepared to encourage the NGOs, the Superintending Engineer, who was supposed to grant the technical sanction, was outright against the very idea of involving NGOs in the irrigation field. In anguish, he raised 60 technical objections to three of the four lift irrigation proposals under his consideration").

Jagawat reveals how he and his group had to raise issues of larger policy. (I narrate: "Another development that took place around that period is also worth sharing, as it pertains to Sadguru's first successful effort in public advocacy for changing a government policy. The community lift irrigation schemes under DPAP provided that 50 per cent of the cost of the scheme would be contributed by the beneficiaries. In principle, Sadguru had no objection to such a cost-sharing requirement. But, it had serious reservations about the rationale of such a policy on the ground that this amounted to injustice to the tribal beneficiaries. I argued that when all kinds of community irrigation systems, large, medium and minor, were supported entirely by the Government, that too, for relatively richer people and regions, there was no justification for the poorest to share half of the cost of the schemes").

We now know if for no other reason but the Asian Development Bank's recent culture that social change requires champions. As Jagawat says: "In 1981, the then Secretary, Rural Development, Gujarat, Anil Shah, visited a couple of lift irrigation schemes. I still vividly remember that I had to persuade him immensely to do that, he felt he had seen many such schemes, and therefore, there was no need for him to see more. Finally, he agreed to visit the schemes and as usual, interacted with the farmers very intensely. He found the schemes were very beneficial to the farmers. From that day onwards, Anil Shah became one of Sadguru's great supporters. On his return to the state capital, Gandhinagar, he talked to the then Finance Minister, Sanat Mehta, about Sadguru's lift irrigations schemes and the need to expand the programme. The Finance Minister wrote a special letter to our organization to undertake 100 more such lift irrigation projects in the district, assuring the availability of necessary funds." He has many interesting but similar vignettes in this book.

He makes the point that in this country when we face a problem, instead of solving it, we try to develop a new structure and scheme replacing the earlier one. "Is it because they do not want to own the responsibility for the failure of their schemes? Or, is it because by winding up the old schemes, the question of inquiring into the causes of the failure of past schemes is automatically eliminated? Or, is it because the ruling party finds it more convenient to replace the scheme than revamping the ongoing one and telling people: "look, old schemes of the previous Government were not good and that is why we instead of improving the ongoing programme are now giving you a new and better scheme."

There have been many hours of glory for Jagawat and he describes them affectionately. In the book he narrates an incident of Somabhai: "Whereas he earned a handsome amount from the nursery, other farmers in the village were suffering from the adverse effects of the drought, particularly, from acute fodder shortage. He decided to give water from his well to the nearby farmers and to provide irrigation to ten acres of the land of twenty farmers almost free of cost only charging for the actual diesel cost." As he rightly says, this is in sharp contrast to the so-called progressive farmers selling drinking water and making huge profit during acute shortage. He also talks affectionately of the tribal farmers Hirjibhai and Nurjibhai with whom he started his rural development work 30 years back and who still bring for him the first harvest of maize cobs.

All in all, the delightful book to be read both for pleasure and profit. I consider it a great privilege to recommend it to the development community.

Dr. Yoginder Alagh

Dr. Yoginder Alagh is an internationally known economist who has served on various important positions in our country such as Minister of State for Planning, Science and Technology, Government of India, Vice Chancellor of Jawaharlal Nehru University, etc.

CHAPTER - 1

Rural India is Real India

India is a land of villages. With more than 700 million people living in over 6,00,000 villages no strategy of development can succeed that neglects rural areas and rural people (Singh, 1999:23).

However, even after more than fifty years of independence, India's villages continue to be poor and backward in terms of basic infrastructure, income levels and employment opportunities. The incidence of both poverty and unemployment is higher in the rural sector than in the urban. For example, in 1999-2000, about 27% of the rural population was below the poverty line as compared to about 24% in urban areas (see Table 1). (These are government figures, which can be contested on the ground that the percentage of population below poverty line may be higher than claimed by the government). In absolute terms, of the total population of about 268 million living below the poverty line in 2001 in the country, 205 million (74%) were in rural areas.

In rural areas, in 1999-2000, the incidence of poverty was the highest among agricultural and other labour, as high as 47% and 29% respectively, followed by those self-employed in non-agriculture and self-employed in agriculture. However, a look at the distribution of the total poor across different groups shows that the largest fraction of the poor in rural areas belong to "agricultural labour" followed by the "self-employed in agriculture" category. There has not been much change in the occupation-wise distribution of the poor in rural areas over the years. Similar is the case for urban areas (Parikh and Radhakrishna 2002: 74).

Table 1: Population Below the Poverty Line

(As per the Expert Group Methodology)

S. No.	Sector	1973-74	1977-78	1983	1987-88	1993-94	1990-2000

Population in Millions							
1.	Rural	261.3	264.3	252.0	231.9	244.0	193.2
2.	Urban	60.0	64.6	70.9	75.2	76.3	67.0
3.	Total	321.3	328.9	322.9	307.1	320.3	260.2
Poverty Ratio (%)							
1.	Rural	56.4	53.1	45.7	39.1	37.3	27.1
2.	Urban	49.0	45.2	40.8	38.2	32.4	23.6
3.	Total	54.9	51.3	44.5	38.9	36.0	26.1

Source: NIRD (2000), Rural Development Statistics, p. 101.

The incidence of poverty varies across household groups based on land ownership status and type of land owned. Around 50% of the rural population belongs to the small farmer group and this group contributes the maximum to aggregate rural poverty — 57.5% of the total poor. Further, incidence of poverty is found to be the highest among small farmers and least among bigger farmers (Parikh and Radhakrishna 2002: 7).

Back to Villages

In view of this, there is a need to regenerate rural life and economy if India is to be seen as seriously interested in an all-round sustainable and equitable development of its citizens. Recognizing this imperative, Mahatma Gandhi had urged people to go "back to the villages". This call needs to be revived, reinforced and translated into action. It requires a fundamental change in the paradigm of development which Western in concept, emphasizes urbanization, industrialization and globalization. A development strategy needs to be adopted that may be based on a particular situation, being open, at the same time, to modern technology.

Barely 40-50 years back in India, the village was the centre of all economic and social activities. And those who had to leave the village for jobs or other compulsions stayed involved in its activities.

Students would come back to the village during vacations to help their parents with farm chores and other activities, marriages would be solemnized in the village and mostly people would come back to the village after retiring.

Gradually but steadily people were caught in the urban web. Most of the educated villagers now leave to settle permanently in the urban centres. They sell their agricultural land and house in the village and sever all ties. Villages pay a heavy price for such permanent migration. As a consequence of this brain drain villages are deprived of the human resources. An educated, versatile, articulate and enlightened leadership becomes unavailable. The history of developed villages or communities is a history of the right kind of leadership — a leadership that can chart out a village'balance route to progress. I once saw a news story on television about a small village in Uttaranchal, which has produced 14 IAS officers, and yet, the village is in shambles. The officers have moved to bigger cities and are not involved in the upliftment of their village.

My Entry into Rural Development

My basic concepts of rural development were formed during my childhood days itself when I used to visit my village in the interiors of Madhya Pradesh. I belong to a village called Ekkalgarh, situated on the banks of River Chambal in Madhya Pradesh. I was appalled by the poverty and misery of its people, despite a reasonably good natural resource endowment. I started searching for ways and means to improve the socio-economic conditions of the villagers using their natural and human resources.

Along with my village background and my intensive training and exposure in the rural development field during my post-graduation at the MS University of Baroda, provided me motivation to get into the field and work for rural people, particularly the poor.

The first opportunity to do so came in 1972, with my appointment as a lecturer in a training institute. The second opportunity, to my surprise and good fortune, came much earlier than expected. Shri Sadguru Seva Sangh Trust (SSST), a charitable organization of the Mafatlal group, organised a massive free eye camp for cataract operations in Dahod in January 1974. My wife and I offered voluntary services at the camp, lasting nearly three weeks. I was assigned the task to transport patients and their attendants. Nearly 20,000 people were to be brought from far away places including nearby districts of Rajasthan and Madhya Pradesh and were to be sent back to their homes as well. It was a massive operation. It seems, in retrospect, that the organizers Arvind Mafatlal, Chairman of Sadguru Seva Sangh, and other directors of Mafatlal Group, were happy with my work. On the concluding day of the camp he said that they were looking for workers like me to join their organization, Sadguru Seva Sangh Trust (SSST), working for rural development. SSST was working in the states of Gujarat, Madhya Pradesh, Maharashtra and Rajasthan. I was appointed Chief Executive Officer of the Dahod project and started working on an honorary basis from January 1974 and full time from 1975. My wife was already working in the same region, and she joined SSST a little later in the year 1977.

I would like to draw the following two major lessons from my experience and observations in my village.

Water is a Catalyst to Development

Poverty in villages may be attributed to the non-utilization of natural resources. Ekkalgarh is on the banks of river Chambal, and yet it does not have enough water for irrigation. To solve the water crisis, some 30 years back, in 1968, villagers thought of installing a lift irrigation scheme on the river. A teacher from our village, Maniraj Singh, took the initiative. He approached the Madhya Pradesh Lift Irrigation Corporation, a body responsible for expanding use of lift irrigation in Madhya Pradesh. The officers at the corporation responded positively and got the lift irrigation cooperative for the village duly registered under the Cooperative Act in 1970. Unfortunately, the corporation, after mismanaging its operations, went into liquidation. The plan of installing a lift irrigation system hung fire.

By this time, Sadguru had developed expertise in lift irrigation and had also installed a few projects in Jhabua, Madhya Pradesh. While working in Jhabua, I realized that my village had been waiting for a similar scheme. My efforts were wasted as the Irrigation Department objected to the proposal. Also local politics hampered my progress; political leaders of a particular party were more interested in lift irrigation projects in other villages on the river Chambal. Failing to obtain the approval and financial support from the state, I approached CAPART. CAPART approved the project, which was duly implemented in 1994-95. The scheme is managed by the community since then. It took 25 years to get the scheme operational.

Delay in development projects comes with a price, which the village communities pay. They are deprived of additional earning and have to undergo mental anguish to get their work done. Can the government and other agencies prevent such deprivation in other villages of this country?

Wasteland Development for Rural Development

I also realized that substantial potential for development existed in the wastelands in Ekkalgarh. The village had more than 200 hectares of wasteland. The valley and ravine lands are extremely rich and fertile. Planting of trees on such a land would be extremely beneficial. In my opinion, if these wastelands were planted with suitable tree species, the village could generate additional income of at least a crore rupees per year, supplementing the income of each of the 100 households in the village, by an average of Rs 1,00,000 annually. It is heartening to know that villagers have now become aware of this potential and some of them have already started planting trees on their wasteland. The others will follow them soon, I hope. Planning is being done to cover entire wastelands with tree cover under the watershed approach.

The development activities taken up in my village have influenced the nearby villages, including the villages on the opposite bank of the river Chambal in the Jhalawar district. At Sadguru, there is an increased demand for similar development in those villages. The political leadership, cutting across the party lines, has shown keen interest in such development-oriented activities.

CHAPTER - 2

Conceptualisation And Evolution Of Sadguru Model Of Rural Development

Basic Concepts and Connotations of Rural Development

"Development" is a subjective and value-loaded concept and hence there cannot be a consensus on its meaning. The term is used differently in diverse contexts. But generally speaking, development may be conceptualized as a set of desirable social objectives or indices, which do not decrease over time. Some of the objectives that are usually included in the set are (Singh, 1999):

- increase in real income per capita (economic growth);
- improvement in distribution of income (equity);
- political and economic freedom; and
- equitable access to resources, education, health care, employment opportunities, and justice.

The term, "rural development" connotes an overall development of rural areas with a view to improve the quality of life. In this sense, it is a comprehensive and multidimensional concept and encompasses the development of agriculture and allied activities, village and cottage industries and crafts, socio-economic infrastructure, community services and facilities, and, above all, the human resources in rural areas. *As a phenomenon,* rural development is the end result of interactions between various physical, technological, economic, socio-cultural, and institutional factors. *As a strategy,* it is designed to improve the economic and social well being of the rural poor. *As a discipline,* it is multidisciplinary in nature representing an intersection of agricultural, social, behavioural, engineering, and management sciences. According to Robert Chambers (1983), "Rural development is a strategy to enable a specific group of people, poor rural women and men, to gain for themselves and their children more of what they want and need. It involves helping the poorest among those who seek a livelihood in the rural areas to demand and control more of the benefits of rural development. The group includes small scale farmers, tenants, and the landless."

The concept of sustainable development, in the present scenario, has become extremely popular in both developed and developing countries of the world. According to the World Commission on Environment, sustainable development is "development that meets the needs of the present without compromising the ability of future generations to meet their own needs" (WCED 1987).

Alternatives Strategies

Many alternative strategies have been put forward by academicians, social reformers and practitioners for rural development and re-building of villages. Numerous programmes are planned and implemented by the government and others for the revival of villages and their economy. Large sums of money are spent every year on villages and the poor. National and international seminars and conferences are held to discuss the problems of rural poverty. But, sadly, the outcome of such programmes and events do not commensurate with the investments made. India is still poor.

Many solutions are offered to revive our villages but few achieve the expected results. A possible solution, according to me, could be the return of people who have migrated from their villages. People need to come back to their villages after retirement and offer the benefit of their experiences and skills to their fellow villagers. This may help in improving the overall living standards of the village.

Return to the villages will also have positive impact on the over-crowded cities and urban centres. It will decongestion these urban areas, reduce pressure on civic amenities like education, health care, transport and communication, law and order maintenance, pollution and crime rate. Besides, in villages, it will restore family, social and cultural relations and improve the village economy.

It is argued that life in villages lacks even basic amenities. It is people who can bring change. Villages in the Anand and Kaira districts of Gujarat are some examples where people have changed their lives drastically. In these districts, NRIs have kept live and continuous relationship with their villages and their prosperity has been transferred to the villages. The villages have proper pucca houses. There are good schools and hospitals, virtually in every village.

In a survey by *India Today*, statistics showed Himachal Pradesh as the most progressive state. One major reason for this development could be that its educated people have settled down in the villages after retiring from service in the army and other sectors. I have come across numerous incidents of army officers and other retired officers becoming sarpanchs and village leaders after their retirement. Obviously, this is going to make huge difference on the progress and quality of life in the villages.

If only transportation infrastructure from villages to the urban centres improves and public transportation system whether in the government hands or in the private is ensured large number of people would commute regularly for their work rather than settling down in the urban centres.

I feel the concept of urbanization should change, bringing urban amenities in rural villages, rather than rural folk migrating to urban centres. This has been recently advocated by our President. Abdul Kalam.

We often talk of the involvement of corporate companies, business houses in rebuilding our villages. But no serious and concrete efforts have been made in this direction. In a hypothetical situation, if 1,000 successful companies take up responsibility to rebuild 10 villages each, it can help 10,000 villages. If 10,000 successful traders help to rebuild five villages each, it may influence 50,000 villages.

Genesis and Evolution of Sadguru Model

The majority of people in India live in a "bio-mass based subsistence economy". In the coming years, India's demand for food, fibre, firewood, fodder, building materials like timber and industrial raw materials will grow by leaps and bounds. Such demands could be effectively met only if we can evolve a highly efficient system for producing all the needed bio-mass which will, at the same time, be ecologically sound and sustainable — not with the help of technologies that produce bumper yields but degrade the natural resources base and thereby jeopardise the livelihoods of future generations. The same holds for other aspects of development like provision of infrastructure and employment generation. We need to evolve a system of managing our natural resources that is sustainable — environmentally, socio-economically, culturally and technologically.

Sadguru's prime project area, Dahod, Gujarat, is predominantly inhabited by Bhils, who are one of the Schedules Tribes of India. In the past, the tribals in this area were dependent on the forest for their livelihood as in other tribal regions as well. When the forests depleted local people slowly took to subsistence farming to eke out their livelihood. Seventy four percent population in Dahod is tribal. In general, the level of literacy in the project area is much lower and the incidence of poverty higher as compared to the non-tribal areas. In any tribal region, below poverty line population ranges from 60-85 %. Due to poverty, the nutrition level of people is very low. Women bear the major workload — they collect fuel-wood and fodder and fetch drinking water and work in the fields. There are no non-farm employment opportunities available in the area. Excessive population growth has aggravated the scarcity of food, fuel-wood, and fodder in the area. People migrate seasonally to urban areas in search of wage-paid jobs to support their families.

Until 1940s, the region was rich in natural resources but the lack of judicious management and fragmented approach of the government to development led to degradation and depletion of the local natural resource base, particularly the forests.

Subsistence farming is practiced under rainfed conditions and crop yields are low and vary widely from year to year depending upon the fluctuations in the rainfall. In the beginning, land holdings were quite large but because of high population growth, particularly among tribals, the land holdings have not only become small but also fragmented. An average land holding has reduced to less than one hectare per household with the average number of land parcels per holding ranging from 2 to 4. Most of the tribals are poor marginal and small farmers.

Community-based natural resources management (NRM) seems to be of great relevance as a strategy for sustainable development of tribal areas in India. Several efforts have been made by both government agencies/departments and NGOs to develop location-specific innovative models/approaches to participatory management of land, water, forests and fisheries. Some of the well-known models developed and adopted in India include the Sukhomajri model of watershed management (Chopra et. al., 1990; Singh, 1995), the Ralegaon Siddhi model of watershed management (Singh, 1995), the Arabari experiment in joint forest management (Singh, 1994, ch. 13), the Van Panchayats of Uttar Pradesh Hills (op.cit. ch. I 1) and the Mohini Water Cooperative Society (op.cit. ch. 9). Based on our assessment of the needs of tribal people drawing lessons from India's experience with NRM-based strategies of rural development, Sadguru also tried to evolve and implement a model of participatory natural resources management in its project area. An integrated approach to natural resources management is being followed with emphasis on community participation, and capacity building and development of people-centered village institutions. This strategy is now known as the Sadguru model of rural development.

The Sadguru Model : An Overview

For any development to take place there must be a driving force. The Sadguru model of development is centered around water —a critical input in the process of agricultural and rural development in all the tribal areas in the country. The underlying premise of the model is that most tribal areas in the country receive adequate rainfall which, if harvested, stored, and utilized properly, can make more productive use of land for agricultural crops and tree plantation in those areas. Given the highly undulating topography of tribal areas and lack of water harvesting and conservation structures, most of the rainwater runs off and gets wasted. What is needed to initiate and foster rural development in such areas is an appropriate institutional arrangement and investment for harvesting, storing, and distribution of water in the larger interest of the local communities. Sadguru adopted a strategy aimed at providing both these critical inputs for agricultural and rural development. It raised the needed funds from various governmental and non-governmental sources including foreign donors and organize the farmers for operating and managing co-operative lift irrigation schemes by motivating and training them.

Communities and natural resources are two basic constituents of rural settings in most of the tribal areas in India and they are inter-dependent and interact with each other. A community plays an important role in determining the use and management of natural resources and *vice versa.* Therefore these two constituents have been treated as the basis of this model. The quality and quantity of natural resources available to a community determine to a large extent the quality of life of people. And the way a community uses and manages its natural resources determines the productivity and sustainability of the resources.

To strengthen the linkages between community and natural resource base, water has been considered the main basis (stem) of this model. Village institutions and community participation play an important dual role of receiving and giving feedback about the ongoing activities and enhancing the sustainability of the model. Programme activities are shown as the main off-shoots of the model while the benefits drawn by the community as fruits of the development.

Thus, the model is built around three major activities, namely, natural resources, mainly water and land, human resources (a proxy for community), and people's institutions. Under water and land resources development, lift irrigation, check dams, watershed development, agro-forestry, joint forest management, agriculture and horticulture are the major activities. Empowering people through training, and provision of technical information and advice constitutes the major intervention for human resource development. Organizing the communities around various land and water resources development projects to improve their livelihood options is the major component of institution building. Training and public advocacy are also used as tools for networking and to influence/policies with a view to replicate the model in similar semi-arid regions. In addition to the above activities, non-farm sources of income and employment such as development of local handicraft, and promoting savings and credit activities are also promoted.

Development of natural resource base through these activities and management of the system by the community itself are the key determinants of sustainable and equitable socio-economic development. This has been observed in the field over the last 30 years over which this model has evolved and has been refined. A diagrammatic representation of the model is presented in Figure 2.1.

Conceptual model of Community Based Natural Resource Management

NM Sadguru Waer & Development Foundation

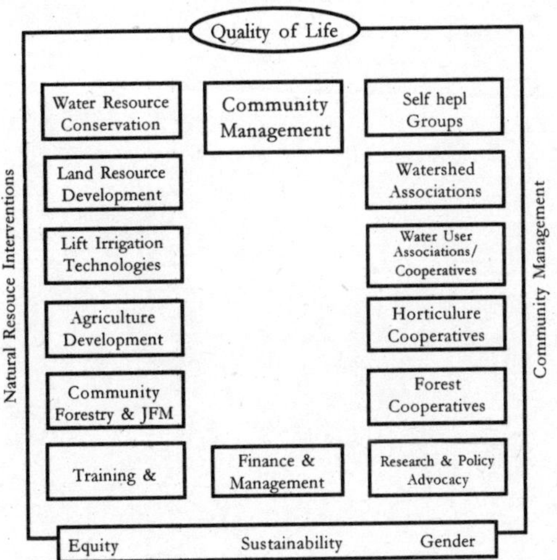

Figure 2.1 : A conceptual representation of the

The model is built on two foundations, namely, water and land resources development and human resource development. These two types of resources are channelised through people's institutions for improving the quality of life of rural people. This is done through a wide variety of income generating activities supported by training and documentation. Besides, public advocacy is also an important component of the model. This is used to influence public policies that are not pro-poor and that are difficult to implement. Sadguru has successfully used advocacy for convincing the State Government and the Central Government about the need for changes in their policies and has got the needed changes incorporated in the revised policies and guidelines.

CHAPTER - 3

Water Resources Development and Management

Water is a finite but renewable natural resource, and, like other natural resources, it is also a free gift of Mother Nature to humankind. Water is essential for survival of all living beings on this planet and so also for socio-economic development of households, communities and nations all over the world. It is also necessary to maintain and enhance biodiversity and quality of environment.

In most of the semi-arid regions of India, inadequate availability of water is the most limiting factor in agricultural and rural development. Those regions receive, on average, 400 mm to 1,000 mm rainfall annually, which if harvested and used judiciously, could support a higher cropping intensity than the existing one. But unfortunately, in the absence of proper and adequate water harvesting structures, most of the surface run-off from the rainfall is lost into the rivers and streams leaving the region perpetually starved of water. Realising this, and based on my assessment of the felt needs of tribals in Dahod district, my organization initiated an innovative experiment in impounding and utilising the rain water and used water as an entry point and as a catalyst for initiating and fostering a number of income generating activities for socio-economic development of tribals in the area.

Water as an Entry Point

Once the tribal area around Dahod was selected by Sadguru for implementing its rural development activities, the first step that was taken was to conduct a socio-economic survey of the area and to find out the felt/priority needs of the people and the potential for development. It was a comprehensive exercise lasting more than 18 months. The method used was similar to the present day PRA exercise. The concept of PRA was not coined in the mid seventies nor the term 'transect walk' was known. Besides, Sadguru was then a one-man organization where I performed all the functions. I resorted to taking walks. Sometimes I would take a bus or use my scooter. During these walks, I interacted with several villagers and their groups, which included village *sarpanchs*, village leaders, youths and anyone around on that day, time and place. Main topics of interactions were their socio-economic conditions, what they thought should be done to improve and what were the potentials for development in the village. I visited more than 200 tribal villages during this exercise. Need for water emerged as the primary concern.

Since Sadguru wanted to work to meet the felt and expressed needs of the people and I never wanted to impose my idea of development, a serious thought was given by the organization to develop water resources to reduce the poverty rampant in the area. Incidentally, enough water was available in the region. The average annual rainfall of about 800 mm was adequate in a normal situation for meeting various needs of local people. The topography of the region was characterized by a large network of drainage systems. There was ample scope for harvesting and utilization of existing water resources and much more for impounding of water. Perhaps, duly recognizing this potential, the Government of Gujarat had constructed several ponds under the scarcity relief programmes year after year. Sadguru staff found such ponds and other water bodies existing in the area helpful in formulating its own strategy and projects. The real challenge for Sadguru staff was to identify and use the most appropriate technology. The commonly used method of flow irrigation or gravity irrigation was not suitable under the existing conditions in the region. Use of lift irrigation technology was identified to be the most suitable option for adoption. This was because the fields were at a higher level than the water resources. This necessitated the lifting of water from its source to be available for irrigation in uplands. Though the modern lift irrigation technology operated with pumps was in practice in India for a long time, it was not yet in common use in the tribal regions, where it suited most. Besides, Sadguru also did not have any experience of water resources development using lift irrigation. But, fortunately for Sadguru, the House of Mafatlals, the sponsor and patron of Sadguru, had resources, expertise and credibility to take up the issue. So they came forward to help Sadguru in setting up lift irrigation projects. Immediately, a search for an expert in lift irrigation system technology was underway. As the lift irrigation technology was widely used in Maharashtra, three top most experts from Maharashtra were identified within 24 hours. V. G. Nalavade finally agreed to help Sadguru in the development of lift irrigation. He was a down-to-earth, hard working, unassuming person. He started his work with Sadguru in 1975 and continues to be associated with Sadguru ever since. Today, Sadguru's lift irrigation systems are among the best in India.

Overcoming the Teething Problem: Mobilizing Funds

Sadguru had no funds to meet the capital cost of lift irrigation schemes. The Mafatlals provided funds for meeting the managerial costs, but not the capital cost. It was decided to seek the needed financial support for the purpose from the Government of Gujarat, as the setting up of community irrigation systems was the responsibility of the Government and the lift irrigation schemes were one of the ongoing programmes of the Government under the Department of Rural Development. The selected region was declared drought prone under DPAP (Drought Prone Area Programme). It was also covered under the Tribal Development Programme of the Government, as it was predominantly inhabited by the tribal community.

Sadguru approached the Department of Rural Development, Gujarat, for financial support for four community lift irrigation systems. The response of the Department was encouraging, as it believed in involving voluntary/non-governmental organizations in the implementation of its programmes. However, the lift irrigation being a technical field, technical sanction was required from the technical department concerned, in this case, the Irrigation Department. In those days, nearly three decades ago, the role of NGOs in irrigation development was neither accepted nor encouraged. The technical department, however, felt that irrigation was their work-area and that NGOs had no business entering the field. They raised several objections to the proposals. All the objections raised on the three proposals were satisfactorily answered by Sadguru. After much convincing we were given the approval.

Another development worth sharing is Sadguru's first successful effort in public advocacy was to help bring about a change in a government policy. The community lift irrigation schemes under DPAP had a provision that 50% of the cost of the scheme would be contributed by the beneficiaries. In principle, Sadguru had no objection to such a cost sharing requirement. But, it had serious reservations about the rationale of such a policy as it felt that this amounted to injustice to the tribal beneficiaries. I argued that when all the community irrigation systems, large, medium and minor, were supported fully by the Government, that too, for relatively richer people and regions, there was no justification for requiring these people to share half of the cost of the schemes. If the poor were to contribute to meeting half of the cost of community systems, then such cost sharing should be uniformly applied at the state and country level for all community irrigation systems. The Secretary, Rural Development, was convinced by this argument. However, as the policy was framed by the Government of India, he advised Sadguru to take up the issue with the Secretary, Rural Development, Government of India. Dr. B. Rudramurthy, Sadguru's Advisor, Rural Development, took up this issue with the Government of India on behalf of Sadguru and convinced the Secretary, Government of India, of the need to change the policy. Accordingly, the policy of cost sharing by the beneficiaries was modified, that is, the government to meet the 100 % of the capital cost of community lift irrigation schemes under DPAP. However, there are conflicting opinions on the policy change and some people argue that the beneficiaries must contribute their share of the cost of lift irrigation systems. I would like to clear it that, Sadguru is also in favour of such a contribution by the beneficiaries. But, such a contribution should be universally collected from the beneficiaries of all the community irrigation systems. In fact, in our opinion, the subsidy for the capital cost should vary from region to region depending on their affordability and financial support could be a one time benefit to be given when the system is created. Irrespective of the opinion of national and international consultants, we opine that if subsidy on capital cost of irrigation is to be discontinued, then it should be done across the board for all projects and it should begin from more developed regions and rich people.

Our problems did not cease with the granting of the technical sanction for three lift irrigation schemes and with the provision where full cost was to be borne by the Government. When the systems were installed, they were the first in the region and people had little confidence in their viability. Also as the operational cost of lift irrigation was much higher in comparison to the flow irrigation system, the farmers were apprehensive about the costs. In Sadguru's first lift irrigation scheme at village Shankerpura, in the first year, only 50 acres were irrigated against the designed command of about 300 acres. But after seeing the results of one season, from the next season, almost full command was irrigated.

The operational cost of community lift irrigation has always been a matter of controversy and has been distorted by misinformation and false propaganda and irrational views held by vested interests and by those ignorant of the operation of lift irrigation systems. Many such people in the Government and outside have always compared the flow irrigation charges with the actual charges levied on the lift irrigation systems. They tend to forget the basic fact that the cost of operation of flow irrigation in our country is much higher than the charges fixed by the government and the flow irrigation systems are heavily subsidized. Whereas in the case of community lift irrigation schemes, no subsidy is available to meet even a small fraction of the operational cost, and therefore, entire operational cost of the scheme whether operated by diesel or electric pumps, is borne by the beneficiaries themselves and their cooperatives. Several studies have revealed that if the Government starts charging the real resource cost of irrigation or even the actual operational cost to the farmers in flow irrigation systems, then the charges would be many times more than the present charges. An important distinguishing feature of community lift irrigation systems is that the beneficiaries pay full operational costs and recovery of water charges is almost 100 % whereas in the case of flow irrigation, water charges are nominal and the recovery is very low — less than 25 % in most cases. Sometimes recovery is as low as 10 %. In fact, running of the flow irrigation system imposes a heavy burden in the form of subsidies on the public, but the Government bears no financial burden with respect to the operational cost of lift irrigation schemes.

Expansion of Lift Irrigation

The first three lift irrigation schemes commissioned in 1976 and 1977 were like an experiment, with everyone watching carefully and critically. The performance of these three schemes, and one more added after four years, convinced everyone about the viability of community lift irrigation schemes and also about the capability of the tribal community to manage successfully such technically sophisticated systems. People, particularly, the Government officers, from both the State and the Central Governments, started visiting these successful tribal lift irrigation schemes. In 1981, the then Secretary, Rural Development, Gujarat, Anil Shah, visited a couple of lift irrigation schemes. He found the schemes were very beneficial to the farmers. Since then, Anil Shah is one of Sadguru's great supporters. On his return to the state capital, Gandhinagar, he talked to the then Finance Minister, Sanat Mehta, about Sadguru's lift irrigations schemes and the need to expand the programme. The Finance Minister also visited the scheme and thereafter in a special letter, asked the organization to undertake 100 more such lift irrigation projects in the district, assuring the availability of necessary funds. However, we felt that we were not fully equipped for such a rapid and relatively massive expansion. We accepted a very modest target of only five projects.

By 1989 we had installed 39 community lift irrigation schemes in the district. The number gave us confidence in our capabilities and at the same time seeing the success of such schemes, farmers' demand for lift irrigation, also increased. However, the State Government policy towards NGOs changed in 1986 and the Government decided to require NGOs to contribute 20 % of the cost of the scheme as their share whenever such schemes were to be implemented by them. This negative policy change restricted the further growth of lift irrigation in the project area. We successfully and single handedly took up the issue of sharing costs by NGOs with the state government and the Government decided to reduce the share from 20 % to 5 % in our case and thereafter for few other select NGOs. As the total cost from the Government was not available due to above policy, we were required to raise the matching contribution from non-governmental sources.

Fortunately, the foreign funding from Aga Khan Foundation and NORAD started flowing in for the programme from the year 1990 onwards. This gave us impetus to expand our lift irrigation and other development programmes. The foreign fund was also utilized for leveraging the funds from the Government and other organizations. From 1994 to 2001, massive foreign funding was available to the organization for the programme activities. Huge Government funding was also availed during above period. As a result, till December 2001, 206 lift irrigation schemes had been installed, a great scaling up along with the scaling up of various other programmes. By December 2004, the numbers of community lift irrigation schemes had reached 243. Each of these schemes designed by our organization has an average designed command of more than 150 acres in one season and about an average of 300 cropping acres for each scheme, which is much higher than the lift irrigation schemes installed by many other NGOs in the country.

15 Years Wait

In the list of lift irrigation projects undertaken in 1993-94, five projects, namely, Chanasar-I, Chanasar-II, Raniyar Kanbi Falia, Tandi and Sampoi are located on the reservoir of the Machhan Nalla Medium Irrigation project of the Government of Gujarat, there was a wait of 15 years before these lift irrigation projects materialized. When the Machhan Nalla reservoir was constructed in 1977, the land of some villages got submerged. The project-affected people lost their most fertile land and shifted slightly away from the submerged area. I approached the then Superintending Engineer (SE) of Machhan Nalla Project with a request to allow Sadguru to construct a few lift irrigation projects on the reservoir for the benefit of these project-affected people. But our request was rejected on the ground that there would be no surplus water. On the basis of the record of all such dams in the region, we argued that there would definitely be surplus water. The Superintending Engineer bluntly replied that we have to wait for 15 years to determine the surplus water.

Finally in 1992, permission to lift water for the above lift irrigation projects was granted and Sadguru put up a total of 12 lift irrigation projects on the above reservoirs benefiting all the project-affected people. This is an example of the apathy of officials and sometimes, of the Government departments. People of the affected region had to wait for 15 long years also lose out on additional income they might have benefited from had the systems been put up in time.

However, since then, in Gujarat, policy towards granting permission to the tribal cooperatives for the reservoirs and canals in the tribal regions has changed. It is more open to such schemes. Sadguru can legitimately claim a credit for such a change in policy.

Community Participation and Management

All the community lift irrigation schemes installed by the organization are fully managed by the community, mostly under the aegis of lift irrigation cooperatives. When the farmers demand a community lift irrigation scheme in their village, they know that the post-construction management would be their responsibility. All the operational functions such as operating the pumps, water distribution, recovery of water charges, conflict resolution and account keeping and administrative chores are looked after by the lift irrigation cooperatives. Since there is no subsidy from any source available for meeting even a fraction of the operational cost, the full operational cost is recovered from the community / users. Two methods are adopted by the cooperatives for levying water charges. One, a fixed flat charge per acre per watering, and two, a fixed charge per hour. It is up to the cooperative concerned to decide which of the two methods is more suitable and convenient to it. By and large, all the lift irrigation cooperatives have performed satisfactorily. Of course, there are certain problems beyond the control of the community which affect the functioning of these cooperatives. They include inadequate power supply and inadequate availability of water during drought years. When droughts occur consecutively for 3 or 4 years, the functioning of lift irrigation cooperatives is severely jeopardized. However, the major strength of these cooperatives is that they bounce back and resume their normal operations in a normal rainfall year after remaining dormant for 3-4 successive years due to the non-availability of water due to the droughts. People have developed the capacity and patience to absorb the shocks of closure of the cooperatives for 3-4 years due to the above-mentioned reasons. This is because they have faith in these lift irrigation schemes and hope that once water is available their schemes would be on track once again. There may be hardly a few other examples in India or elsewhere in the world, when an enterprise bounces back to its normal operations after shutting operations for 3-4 years. The tribal community and the robust irrigation system must be given full credit for coming out of such serious situations time and again. Indian farmers have learned to cope with consecutive drought years and rebuild their agriculture once again when monsoon is normal. They do not panic in the drought situation, hoping all the time that the next year would be a normal one.

General Scenario of Lift Irrigation Schemes in the Tribal Regions

Lift irrigation is the most suitable irrigation method for the tribal regions in our country, characterized by undulating topography. Based on this fact, large numbers of community lift irrigation schemes have been installed in different tribal regions of our country in last 25-30 years. Many tribal districts have each hundreds of community lift irrigation schemes installed. Unfortunately, however, about 90% of the community lift irrigation schemes in the tribal regions have become defunct. Most of the community lift irrigation schemes installed by the Government and the contractors in the tribal districts of Gujarat, have also failed. Similar is the case of community lift irrigation schemes in the tribal districts like Banswara, Dungarpur and other tribal districts in Rajasthan. Jhabua district of Madhya Pradesh boasts of having more than 1,000 community lift irrigation schemes. In a recent study, however, it was found that 50 % of them were defunct and remaining 50 % operated with about 35 % of the designed command. Incidentally, each community lift irrigation scheme in Jhabua installed by DRDA under a massive crash programme, has an average a designed command of about 35 acres only. Considering the small size of each lift irrigation scheme in Jhabua, combined with the fact that only 50 % of them are functional, that too, at 35 % of the designed command capacity, the actual irrigation coverage under the 1,000 lift irrigation schemes comes to less than one per cent of the cultivated area of the district. This situation exposes that 1,000 lift irrigation schemes in Jhabua district have not made any significant contribution to the development of irrigation in that district. In view of this, the sooner the Government and others realize this fact and learn from this experience, the better would be for the backward tribal districts like Jhabua. As case in the point, once when I met a senior officer in Madhya Pradesh government and expressed our desire to expand our water development programme in Jhabua he cut me short and said that Jhabua has reached a saturation point in water resource development. I was startled as this was not the case at all. Neither was he interested in a dialogue. Another issue that I have a problem with government officials is accusing the tribals of disinterest and their incapability in handling these systems as an excuse for failed schemes.

In Box 3.1 includes a portion from the Annual Report of Sadguru Foundation for 1998, dealing with the issue of blaming the tribals for the flopped lift irrigation schemes.

Box - 3.1 Please do not blame the Tribals

In the tribal regions of various states like Bihar, Gujarat, Madhya Pradesh, Maharashtra, Rajasthan, large number of community lift irrigation systems have been installed by the Government. Most of these schemes are not functioning. In fact, most of them have become defunct and remaining few are not operating well. In the Parliamentary debate a few months back, a Member of Parliament from Bihar (now Jharkhand) informed the House that more than 300 lift irrigation schemes installed in his district were not functioning. Whenever in the Government Forum this non-functioning of lift irrigation schemes in tribal regions is discussed, invariably various adverse remarks against the tribals are made. "Tribals are not interested in such schemes". "They are lazy and do not want to work." "They do not have the capacity to manage such schemes." "They have no unity to manage such community schemes." "They do not want to pay electricity bills." "They want everything free." All sorts of blames are passed on to the tribals for the non-functioning of hundreds and perhaps thousands of lift irrigation schemes in the tribal regions of our country.

With the experience of 30 years of working with the tribals, vis-à-vis Lift Irrigation Schemes, we do not support any of the above adverse remarks against the tribals. We have seen large numbers of schemes not functioning and have also discussed the reasons with the tribals for such non-functioning. Very clearly and unrefutably, the blame for non-functioning of these schemes lies somewhere else, but, not with the tribals. If the system installed is not of required standard quality, it would never function whether it is to be managed by the tribals or the non-tribals. In a large number of defunct schemes, even the successful trials of the schemes had not taken place and even not for once the water was released in the fields in such schemes. How can people take up the responsibility of such schemes, when they have never seen water coming out of such schemes? First give them a full proof quality system, and then only expect the community to own the responsibility of management. The tribal people are the poorest lot in our country and they know that the lift irrigation is extremely beneficial to them, and therefore, they would do everything to manage it properly, provided the system is technically and operationally sound. If a system is sound, it would automatically generate confidence among the tribals and they are certainly going to manage it successfully as demonstrated in more than 200 tribal lift irrigation schemes of Sadguru across three States of Gujarat, Madhya Pradesh and Rajasthan. It is not just to blame the tribals for the commissions or omissions of others.

We should stop blaming the tribals, identify the culprits who have made a mess of the lift irrigation systems and ensure that in future every system is technically sound. If this is done, we can promise on behalf of the tribals that they would manage the systems successfully.

Besides, technically sound irrigation systems, the tribals also require some material inputs and training for management of these systems and also extension services for better agricultural practices, and suitable cropping pattern necessary to make the lift irrigation viable and profitable. The organization ensures the provision of such inputs to the tribal cooperatives and their federation.

I must emphasize that all lift irrigation projects are viable and profitable if adequate water is available and adequate power supply is ensured. Even with 8-10 hours power supply in a day, most of our lift irrigation schemes achieve 80% or higher of the designed command. There are large numbers of impact studies of our lift irrigation scheme, revealing that the yields and incomes of the farmers have gone up four times to nine times the levels before the installation of such systems. For example, in a recent study conducted under the auspices of IWMI-TATA Research Project, in one hamlet of Mahudi village in Dahod district, Gujarat, the total crop production in the hamlet before lift irrigation and other interventions was only about 82 metric tonnes annually but after the introduction of lift irrigation and other programmes, the total production had gone up to 900 metric tonnes, a phenomenal and more than nine times increase in production. In another village, Mota Dharola in Dahod district, the gross earning of the village before lift irrigation was about Rs. 1.2 million (Rs. 12 lakhs) annually and after lift irrigation it had gone up to about Rs. 10.04 million (Rs. one crore four lakh) annually, almost nine times increase in gross earnings, which includes increased income from agriculture as well as from increased milk production in the village on account of irrigation (milk worth about Rs. 26 lakh is now produced annually in that village, as against Rs. 4 lakh worth of milk produced before lift irrigation). Such amazing results are available in many lift irrigation schemes, supported by various impact studies by the external evaluators from time to time.

Resolving the Electricity Problem

One of the major problems that the lift irrigation schemes have faced is that of inadequate power supply. We know this is a national problem and virtually every state has this problem. Earlier our lift irrigation schemes were designed for 16-hours-a-day power supply situation. Now in view of the uncertain and inadequate power supply position, the schemes are designed for 12 hours of power supply a day. When 12 hours of power supply a day is not available, obviously the achievement is affected. Of course, with some cropping pattern changes requiring less intensive irrigation, the normal level of achievement could be maintained. This approach helps in achieving a reasonable coverage in all our schemes, when water is no problem. The situation of power supply varies in different states, where we have been operating. Situation is reasonably tolerable in Gujarat, where our schemes do get power supply for 10-12 hours a day. Situation in Rajasthan is also not that bad as in Banswara our schemes get about 8-10 hours of power supply every day and in Jhalawar we got about six hours supply in 2002-2003 Rabi, which was apparently not enough, but, improved to 8 hours a day in Rabi 2003-04 which helped a lot in achieving good irrigation. Situation in Madhya Pradesh is the worst among all of the three states. In my opinion, the management of Electricity Boards is of great importance when power deficit is a common phenomenon, and yet, one state manages better than others. For power situation in Madhya Pradesh, the State government itself has made a mess. For a few years, agriculture power up to the connection of 5 HP was free. People grossly misused this free power by installing 4 or 5 motors of 5 HP each on the same well.

We know we have to live with this situation of shortage of power supply. What we are more concerned about is the tariff system. It is irrational to charge for the period when schemes are not operating. Also, when the minimum guaranteed power supply is not given, how can any agency charge the minimum tariff? A clause of minimum tariff has to be linked with the minimum power supply. The respective electricity boards can raise the power tariff, but they cannot just charge for the period, when schemes were not operational or levy the minimum charges without giving minimum power.

Also, flat rate system of tariff based on horse power is not suitable in our tribal regions where mostly water sources are not perennial. Our schemes usually operate for four months during Rabi season, and therefore, a tariff system based on the actual use of power is suitable for our schemes. When this system is adopted, there shall be no minimum charges, particularly, for the period when either electricity is not available or electricity is not availed by agriculturists. In a state like Gujarat, powerful farm lobby is fighting with the Government for adoption of the flat rate per horse power system as it enables them to use as much power as possible and to sell their water. This system is both anti-efficiency and anti-equity. Besides, it has led to the over-extraction of groundwater in many areas in Gujarat, particularly north Gujarat and Saurashtra regions. But, farm lobby is too strong in these regions and the Government tends to succumb to this powerful lobby. Whereas our tribal farmers lobby is too weak to fight for a just and fair system of power tariff based on actual use. Ideally, two parallel systems - flat rate per horsepower and variable rate per unit and metered based for power used, need to co-exist to satisfy the strong farm lobby and to meet the genuine demand of the poor tribals. Such parallel systems are prevalent in Gujarat and they must continue in the interest of poor tribal people who do not have perennial irrigation.

There is also a strong case for ensuring adequate power supply to the tribal agriculturists on the ground that better regions have many alternatives to the people for livelihood such as the industrial development, trade and commerce, service sector, etc. Whereas in the tribal regions such options for livelihood are not available, and therefore, tribal areas require special attention and special treatment in power supply policy. This is a case which needs to be taken up by the tribal leaders and the high powered Schedule Tribes Commission.

Surface Water Harvesting: Construction of Check Dams

In the beginning of the organization, we developed small-scale community lift irrigation projects on already existing water sources like lakes, rivers, canals, etc. After following this approach for some time, we found that it was necessary to harvest and impound water both for supporting some existing lift irrigation schemes and also for installing new lift irrigation schemes on various sources. The region with more than 800 mm of annual rainfall and full of drainage systems offers potential for harvesting surface water, mainly through small scale masonry weirs. An experimental beginning in this direction was made in 1989 and from 1990 onwards this programme of surface water harvesting structures — check dams — got impetus. First few such check dams were supported by CAPART, matched by foreign funds. Like our community lift irrigation schemes, this programme also got impetus from 1994 onwards when substantial foreign funding started coming from the European Commission through the Aga Khan Foundation. During the last 14 years from 1990 to March 2004, 248 masonry weirs have been constructed in our project areas in Gujarat, Rajasthan and Madhya Pradesh. An important feature of our masonry weirs — check dams is their size, which is relatively much bigger in comparison to the check dams constructed by the Government and other NGOs in the region. Most of the check dams constructed by the Government and NGOs do not store even one mcft of water, whereas most of our check dams, store between 5-15 mcft each and in some cases the storage capacity is about 20 mcft and more. In case of recently constructed check dams in Jhalawar, Rajasthan, under the centrally sponsored SGSY Special project, the capacity ranges from 35 mcft to 90 mcft. Such big size and storage capacities of the check dams are suggestive of technical competency of our organization. As for the quality of these structures, none of them have been washed away even in abnormally high rainfall years and floods. The 267 check dams constructed by Sadguru, in terms of their size and capacity, are equivalent to more than 1,000 check dams usually constructed by the Government and other NGOs. The fact that these check dams of Sadguru store more than 1000 mcft of water speaks on their size as well as total storage created, which provide immense benefit to the people around such water bodies.

Another important feature of our check dams is that the series of check dams are constructed at an appropriate interval on the same rivers and rivulets. This approach serves a double purpose. First, the source becomes perennial and secondly, every village gets its own share of the water stored, as the entire river/rivulet is full of water due to the series of check dams constructed on it at the end of monsoon when gates are closed. In this approach, neither upstream nor downstream villages are deprived of water. So far 45 such rivers and rivulets have been made perennial, having water round the year in normal years. Prior to such series of check dams, rivers used to dry up. The flow of water in the river would stop after November in most cases and after December in all cases. A real beauty of this approach is that due to the water stored for such a long period, base flow improves and even if river flow discontinues, the downstream check dams are recharged on account of improved base flow.

Another tangible benefit from such series of check dams is recharging of groundwater in the adjacent areas. Such recharging of ground water is observed from 2 to 4 meters, in a radius of at least 500 meters around the water harvesting structures created on the rivers and rivulets. Often when there is no water in such check dams, there is sufficient water in the open dug wells around the check dams. Sometimes some people criticize the drying up of check dams or the check dams not holding water round the year. The fact is that even if a particular check dam holds water only for 2-3 months after the monsoon, such storage helps greatly in recharging the adjacent ground water. Therefore, storage of water even for a shorter period of time is also beneficial. There are villages in our project where on a small nalla very small structures are constructed at appropriate intervals. These very small structures are masonry in some cases and some are gabion structures with loose stones and wires mesh. Water remains in such small structures on small nalla hardly for two months after the monsoon. But this storage of water for such a short period of time recharges the adjoining wells sufficiently to make these wells perennial for drinking and irrigation purposes. In village Rozam of our project, about 250 horticulture plots and equal numbers of floriculture plots have come up on account of a large number of wells recharged by a small surface structure on a nearby water source. Water is a wonderful thing like magic and even small scale water harvesting structures produce magical results and impacts.

My organization has also offered an example of assured drinking water during drought years by constructing open dug wells just below the check dams. This is an innovative approach. With the expansion of check dams every where in our country, particularly, in the western part of our country, if this approach of construction of open dug wells downstream of the check dams is implemented, there would never be a drinking water shortage even during the successive drought years in those villages where such wells are constructed near the check dams.

The Central Ground Water Board, Gujarat region, has openly endorsed, through measurements, the increase in groundwater in the project area of Sadguru in Dahod and Jhalod. Elsewhere in Gujarat and other states, where water table has been fast depleting to a crisis stage, this increase in groundwater table in Sadguru's project area not only substantiates the success of Sadguru's approach, but, it also provides motivation to other agencies to work in a similar manner to get the similar results.

The role of water as a catalyst of rural development is illustrated through a case study in a tribal village in Gujarat. (Box 3.2)

Box – 3.2

A case study was conducted in a tribal village, Shankerpura, in Dahod, Gujarat. The area is semi-arid and has an annual rainfall of between 400 and 1,000 mm. Most rainfall is concentrated in three months from July to September. The topography is undulating. The total population of the village is about 1,800 and the geographical area covers approximately 588 hectares (ha.). Every household has some land and all households belong to the bhil tribe.

In 1976, Sadguru constructed a small check dam across a river near the village to impound the runoff. It also installed a water-lifting device to distribute water to farmers' fields in the village. Irrigation was provided to approximately 120 ha. of land; some 148 families, who had land in the project's command area, benefited. In addition, the number of private wells increased from 2 to 80.

By the year 2000-2001, the total area under irrigation had increased to 260 ha and all households had access to irrigation. Many of the farmers had terraced and leveled their fields to make them suitable for irrigation. This was carried out under the intensive watershed development schemes funded by the Government of Gujarat and Sadguru. The project is now owned, operated and managed by a cooperative society of irrigators which was developed by Sadguru with full participation of the users.

The project has also had an impact of the environment. Between 1976 and 2001 the total number of trees in the village increased from 100 to over 5,00,000. A survey in 1993 revealed that tree plantation was a highly profitable activity for farmers in the village. This has led to more houses being built and more employment. The rate of seasonal migration has fallen from 75 % in 1976 to about 15 % in a normal monsoon year. The number of school going children has increased, and the literacy rate in the village has risen from 17 % in 1981 to 45 % in 1991. The assured income from trees and irrigated crops has served to provide tree growers with an informal insurance against the adverse effects of droughts and other natural ®asters.

Some Special Features

Sadguru has been quite innovative in its approach and work. Following is a brief description of some of its special features:

Speedy Execution: The design and quality workmanship of Sadguru's water resources projects, both the community lift irrigation systems and check dams, are universally appreciated. With these two aspects of sound design and quality workmanship, another extremely important dimension of our water resources development is the speed with which such projects are executed and completed. For example, a lift irrigation scheme designed to irrigate about 250-300 acres and costing about Rs. 20-25 lakh has been completed in less than three months. As it is a seasonal activity, large numbers of such lift irrigation schemes are implemented at a time and around 15 or more such schemes are executed and completed in less than six months. Similarly, relatively bigger check dams, as described earlier in this chapter, are also completed in record time and at speeds. A small check dam on a small nalla is completed in less than 40 days. A check dam on relatively bigger source - river - costing Rs. 20-25 lakh is completed in three months. Huge check dams on huge rivers like Kshipra and Chambal of Madhya Pradesh and Rajasthan, were constructed in about six months time. Five such huge check dams on river Chambal and river Kshipra, each costing Rs. 50 lakh to Rs. 90 lakhs have been completed simultaneously within seven months. This speed and the high quality of works could be attributed to the technical competency of our staff and the cooperation and response of the community. Both the sizes and the speed of our water resources projects are unmatched, at least in the NGO sector. In the Government sector, the projects of the same size are executed at half of our speed.

Many people fail to appreciate the importance of completion of such projects with great speed and in time. A community lift irrigation scheme of 300 acres command and costing about Rs. 20 lakh, when completed and commissioned in three months, would generate benefits worth about Rs. 18 lakh to the farmers in its command in one season of 3-4 months and in one year with double cropping, the benefits could be around Rs. 30 lakh. If the same project takes two years for its completion, farmers may be deprived of the benefit amounting to Rs. 50-60 lakh or even more if the scheme is perennial and cropping pattern is more profitable. In fact, I myself learnt the value of timely completion from my association with a corporate company in the beginning of my career. I was sitting in a corporate office when the negotiations between the construction company and the chairman of the corporate company and senior officers took place on the construction of huge industrial shades of the industrial unit costing about Rs. seven crores. Three top most builders with high reputation were called for the negotiations, ignoring the tenders of some builders who had quoted lower amount in their bids, but, had no proven reputation of the work involved. When the negotiations were over and the contract for work was awarded to one construction company the chairman offered to pay to the company 10 % more of the amount approved if the work was completed six months before the target time and 5 % more of the amount if the work was completed three months before the schedule. I did not understand this logic of offering higher amount. When I raised this query with one of the senior officers of the company, who was close to me, he said, the reason was very simple. If the work is completed six months in advance, the company will produce the goods worth about Rs. 2 crores every month and thereby Rs. 12 crores in six months. The logic impressed me. In my work in the NGO sector, I also believe that even if it costs a little more, because of market conditions during specific season or period, a speedy completion of a project ahead of the target date would offset such higher costs, if any. For example, certain construction materials like sand, rubbles, gravel and even cement are relatively cheaper during certain off seasons like monsoon period. Most of the people would wait for such off season to buy cheaper material, ignoring the benefits of early completion. We have different approach giving much more importance to the speed in completion.

Cost Effectiveness: From the very beginning, we have faced constant criticism that the cost of our water resources projects — lift irrigation schemes and check dams — were higher in comparison to the costs of similar works done by Government and other NGOs. All such comparisons of the cost are irrational and baseless. We cannot compare two un-equals. In other words, the comparison would be relevant if everything such as the size, and quality were equal. There cannot be a valid comparison of the cost of building of a 100 square-meter structure and that of a 300 square-meter even if the quality of the material were the same. Similarly, there cannot be a comparison between community lift irrigation with the command of less than 50 acres and that of more than 200 acres. And yet, some people in the Government instigated by the contractors and vested interests resorted to such senseless comparisons time and again. I remember there was an Assembly question in Madhya Pradesh Assembly inquiring about the cost of the lift irrigation schemes constructed by DRDA in Jhabua and those constructed by our organization in that district. The question asked was: Why is it that the average cost of DRDA's lift irrigation schemes was around Rs. one lakh whereas the cost of those executed by our organization, Sadguru Foundation, was about Rs. ten lakh each. Average pumping capacity of DRDA schemes was between 5 HP to 10 HP, whereas the average pumping capacity of Sadguru's schemes was 50 HP and more. There was a vast difference in the diameters and length of pipelines. While in the DRDA lift irrigation schemes, the pipeline diameter was very small and the length of pipe was barely 200 meters. In Sadguru's schemes, the diameters were markedly bigger and the length of total pipeline was more than 3,000 meters each. Besides these obvious differences, various types of valves required for different mechanical functions, and large numbers of outlets with civil works were also altogether missing in the DRDA schemes whereas in Sadguru's schemes such valves and outlets were provided in requisite numbers. Similarly, the average command area of DRDA schemes was 35 acres each whereas the average command area of Sadguru's schemes was 150 acres each. The major differences in the cost of lift irrigation schemes are caused by the differences in the height of the head and the length of rising mains. Sadguru schemes have much higher head and very lengthy rising mains and main pipe lines required to take the water to higher height and greater length from the source. There is therefore, no basis for any comparison.

Let us see one actual example. In the year 2000 our organization submitted a proposal for constructing a check dam at Antersuba village in Dahod district. Incidentally, at the same site, the Government's Minor Irrigation Division also proposed a check dam. The funding department, the Tribal Development

Department, was baffled when both the proposals were put up to it for funding. The funding department also found that the cost of Sadguru's check dam was double the amount proposed by the Government. The Department officials went in details of various aspects of the two proposals and extracted the following facts and figures for comparisons between two proposals (Table 3. 2)

Table 3.2 : Certain facts and figures about the Sadguru and the Government proposals for constructing a check dam

Particular/ Description	Government	Sadguru
Length of dam	48.00 meters	75.30 meters
Height of dam from ground	1.50 meters	3.50 meters
Foundation depth	1.50 meters	2.50 meters
Bottom width of the check dam	4.50 meters	5.00 meters
Type of shutter	RCC niddles	M S shutters
Total quantity of masonry construction	200 cum	800 cum
Total water storage capacity	12360.69 cum	49442.76 cum
Total cost (Rs. lakh rounded off)	8.00	16.00

The following facts were revealed by the comparison:

1. The volume of construction work proposed by Sadguru was almost four times higher than the one proposed by the Government;
2. Sadguru's cost of construction was double the one proposed by the Government; and
3. Importantly, Sadguru's check dam was to store four times more water than the one proposed by the Government.

The above detailed comparisons carried out by the Government Department itself opened the eyes of every one. The District Committee, which also included a representative of the Minor Irrigation Department, decided in favour of Sadguru's proposal as it was more cost effective and more beneficial.

It is also an established fact by now that the average cost of the construction of Sadguru's check dams ranges from Rs. one lakh to 1.5 lakh per mcft water, whereas that of the Government-constructed ones is much more than Rs. five lakh per one mcft. These comparative figures were revealed by the Chief Engineer of Irrigation Department, Gujarat. Yet, at the lower levels of hierarchy of the Irrigation Department, baseless and undue comparisons are made and misinformation spread. Such spurious comparisons are made time and again and we have to defend our position every time.

In terms of cost effectiveness, Sadguru's case is very strong, if the quality of structures is taken into account and if someone tries to find out and compare the number of the check dams of the Government that have been washed away or severely damaged with the number of Sadguru's check dams that have been washed away. Such comparisons would reveal that none of the Sadguru's structures have been washed away, whereas many the government-built ones have met that fate. This is despite the fact that quite a few of the Sadguru's check dams are very large and are constructed on large rivers.

Fortunately, there is now all-round appreciation of our work, quality and speed at the higher level of the Irrigation Department. This appreciation and support of higher officers have encouraged us to improve our performance further and expand our scaling up effort. This also has enabled Sadguru to develop water resources potential to the extent of about 90,700 acres of the command and about 1,80,000 of cropping acres in its project areas in the three States, an achievement unmatched in the NGO sector.

Potential for Replication in other Areas

The tribal regions have great potential for similar development in water resources field through small scale lift irrigation and water harvesting structures including ground water recharging. On a conservative estimate based on satellite imageries and the existing network of rivers and rivulets in the central- western tribal regions in India extending over eight states, namely, Bihar, Jharkhand,

Orissa, Madhya Pradesh, Chattisgarh, Maharashtra, Gujarat and Rajasthan, there is potential for constructing around 50,000 water harvesting structures - masonry check dams of varying sizes for storing rain water and for 20,000 community lift irrigation schemes in these regions, each having a command ranging from 100 acres to 200 acres. Both these programmes may result in developing irrigation for about 1.20 crores acres of about 60 lakhs households in the above tribal regions.

Water resources should be developed in the tribal regions. Lift irrigation technology can help the local people in the vicinity of big reservoirs by offering irrigation. What is usually ignored by our planners of the big irrigation systems is that they don't bother about the fate of upstream and downstream people of such big systems. In fact, many irrigation engineers do not permit the construction of even small check dams upstream or downstream of big systems. This is a totally and grossly wrong approach. There should be a series of small structures upstream and down stream of the big systems so that people can enjoy riparian rights all along the length of rivers involved in real sense. Such small structures would hardly affect the reservoirs of big systems. Suppose 50 such small structures are constructed upstream of a big system, altogether impounding about 2,500 mcft of water. This is a negligible share of the total storage capacity of the big system. Similarly, if a series of small structures are constructed downstream of a big system, it may benefit large numbers of villages. Such small structures downstream could be recharged by releasing a negligible portion of water from the big reservoir upstream. This approach may also do away the necessity of constructing lengthy canals almost parallel to the river in downstream as people downstream could use water from such small structures. This approach would also help in decentralization of irrigation systems through small independent systems that are managed by local villagers. Now, when we are considering a mammoth proposal to interlink India's major rivers, we need to adopt this approach. After local seasonal rivers are revived through the release of water from the big reservoirs, linking of rivers could be the second step wherever feasible and practical. Often the government engineers argued that small structured upstream of big system may not allow post monsoon flow to big system. I think, this is injustice to upstream people as it is violation of riparian rights of the upstream villagers. Let big system depend on monsoon flow which is fully available to such system including high flood water, and post monsoon flow may be used by small systems bringing in equity and establishing riparian rights of all villages. Also, several structures upstream, base flow will improve. Similarly, the downstream of big system series of small structures could be constructed which may get overflow of big system as well as benefit of return flow from canal network. The above approach would make the rivers perennial, whereas in the existing approach, the rivers dry up both upstream and downstream of the big system. The irrigation planners have to change their approach in the larger benefit of all.

In water sector, we need to develop a comprehensive and integrated approach in which there is a room for big, medium and small projects. Approaches and programmes should be integrated, supplemented and complement each other. The water situation in India is serious, rather critical, but, a well planned and appropriate approach may help us in meeting the future challenges successfully.

CHAPTER- 4

From Water to Watershed

The Central and the State governments in India have now realized the need to improve the management of land, water, and forest resources and have initiated a number of measures to achieve this. Some of the important measures include the establishment of a National Land Use and Wastelands Development Council with Prime Minister as its Chairperson, announcement of a second revised National Water Policy, and a National Forest Policy, and launching of a National Watershed Development Project for Rainfed Areas. What is needed, however, is an integrated policy for management of land, water and forest resources on watershed basis.

In this chapter, I first briefly describe the watershed approach to management of natural resources and its evolution and applications in India, then describe the Sadguru approach to watershed development and management and its impact through a case study and finally distill lessons from our experience with watershed development projects.

The Watershed Approach

A watershed may be defined as an area from where rainwater is drained through a common outlet into a water body such as a river, a rivulet, a tank, or a lake. The watershed has a clear conceptual identity in hydrology, physical geography, and other natural sciences. The use of this term in social sciences is of rather recent origin. The term is often used synonymously with two other words, namely, basin and catchment. The terms "basin" and "catchment" are generally used to imply drainage areas of large river systems such as the Ganga, the Brahamputra, and the Narmada whereas the term "watershed" usually implies drainage area of small rivers or rivulets, tributaries of rivers, streams, ponds, lakes, and nallas.

Basically, a watershed is a hydrologic unit which, in view of the interdependence of its natural and human resources, is ideally suited for natural resource planning the basic unit for planning and management of land, water, and other resources of the watershed. The approach is holistic and multidisciplinary and is a practicable approximation of the systems approach. It enables the planners and managers to consider together various physical, biological, socio-cultural, economic and institutional factors operating within a watershed and its surrounding environment and formulate a comprehensive and integrated watershed development plan to achieve specific social objectives.

In a watershed, natural and human resources are all interdependent and interact with one another. This gives rise to the problem of externalities. For example, soil and water conservation in a watershed requires the participation of all the land owners having land in the watershed in the form of adoption of recommended soil and water conservation measures. In a nutshell, all uses of all natural resources irrespective of whether they are owned privately or publicly are interdependent and require co-operation of all the resource users for internalizing / minimizing the externalities involved. This is best achieved when planning and management of natural resources, especially common pool resources, is done on watershed basis and the resources are managed by their users who are organized into a formal association preferably a co-operative society (Singh, 1994).

The Evolution of Watershed Approach in India

In India, the Damodar Valley Corporation first adopted integrated treatment of all categories of land on watershed basis as early as 1949. But this isolated experiment, though laudable, failed to create an impact at the national level. It was only in 1974 when the watershed approach was first adopted on a significant scale by the Government of India (GOI) under the Centrally-sponsored "Scheme of Soil Conservation in the Catchments of River Valley Projects". In 1982, the GOI, under the auspices of the Indian Council of Agricultural Research (ICAR) sanctioned 46 model watershed projects to be implemented in the dry-land areas of the country. These projects were implemented by the State governments through their Agriculture Departments and technical back up provided by the All India Coordinated Research Project for Dry-land Agriculture (AICRPDA), the Central Research Institute for Dry-land Agriculture (CRIDA), and the Central Soil and Water Conservation Research and Training Institute. The CRIDA and AICRPDA scientists were responsible for monitoring of 30 of these model watershed projects.

In July 1986, the Union Ministry of Agriculture and Rural Development launched the National Watershed Development Project for Rainfed Areas (NWDPRA) as a Centrally-sponsored scheme. It covered 99 districts in 16 states in the country. The criteria for selection of districts were: (1) the annual rainfall should be 500-1125 mm; and (2) the irrigated area should be less than 30 percent of the cultivated area. The project had been taken up on watershed basis. The main objective of the project was to optimally utilise the available rainwater and minimize the risk of crop failure. The project was financed by the Government of India to the extent of 100 per cent.

Watershed development is one the thrust areas of the Department of Agriculture and Co-operation, Union Ministry of Agriculture and the Ministry of Rural Development in the Tenth Plan. Besides the ICAR projects, and NWDPRA, there are many other watershed development projects funded by international donors currently underway in different states of India.

Present Status of Watershed Development Programmes

The unsatisfactory and poor performance of most of our rural development programmes including the watershed development programme has resulted in perpetuation of rural poverty and degradation of natural resources. This was well comprehended by C. H. Hanumantha Rao Committee in its report. Based on the recommendations of this Committee, the Government of India, Ministry of Rural Development, formulated a Participatory Watershed Development programme and implemented the same from the year 1995 onward. The ultimate objective of this new programme was to promote and achieve sustainable economic development of the village community within the micro watershed through various interventions around land and water resources and to achieve restoration of ecological balance, keeping in mind the sustainable use of such natural resources. In fact, watershed development encompasses all natural and human resources and various activities relating to them. It is a concept, which on proper implementation can transform the lives and ecology of the watersheds concerned on sustainable basis. Watershed should have been adopted as a unit for natural resources planning and development from the very beginning of planned era in India.

The latest and ongoing watershed development programme Launched in 1995 has been well conceived and truly appropriate for our rural development. It has immense potential to transform the lives of rural poor and to restore the rural ecology and eco-system.

Though the watershed programme is a well-designed programme with tremendous potential, given our poor record of implementation of development programmes in the past and the present scenario characterized by deteriorating moral and ethical values and norms, one is not sure whether this programme will be successful or this programme will be more successful than previous ones. Once again, it may turn out to be the same story of a good programme implemented badly and as a result not producing the intended impacts. Already there are signs, in fact reports, which are not encouraging. Several short coming and deficiencies have been observed in the implementation of this programme. A few of them are listed below:

- In a large number of cases the Project Implementation Agencies are not selected on merit basis. Consequently, unscrupulous organizations are selected as implementing agencies, making mockery of the programme;

- Like other programme, this programme is also becoming target oriented, in which the achievement of physical and financial targets has become more important than the quality of the outcome;

- In many cases, the programme interventions are not technically sound;
- In most of the cases, qualified and trained Watershed Development Teams (WDT) as prescribed in the programme guidelines are conspicuously absent;
- In a large number of cases, even the District Rural Development Agency officials are neither well trained nor well motivated to guide and monitor this important programme; and
- In several States where the programme is predominantly implemented through Panchayati Raj Institutions (PRIs), the performance is worse as PRIs and people associated with the implementation are not as well trained and skilled as the Government functionaries and NGO personnel. (This situation should serve as warning to the Government for Hariyali scheme, which is to be mainly implemented by PRIs).
- It seems the Government considers this programme as a welfare or charitable work, with no accountability in performance.

At political level, there is no real appreciation of this programme that it is an economic development programme and the results must commensurate with the investments.

Sadguru's Approach in Watershed Development

Most of the tribal areas in India are characterized by high incidence of poverty ranging from 60-85% of the population, undulating topography and consequently higher rate of soil erosion, a high proportion of degraded forest and revenue lands, recurrent droughts, depleting groundwater aquifers and scarcity of drinking water. Sadguru realized fairly early after its inception that under such conditions, watershed approach is most appropriate for conservation of soil and water, restoration of ecological balance, and providing sustainable livelihoods to local people. The approach needs to be adopted on a significantly larger scale through such areas; a few successful interventions here and there will not do. Our future depends on robust eco-systems, which in turn require well-developed and well-maintained watersheds.

Sadguru's perception of watershed development is slightly different from the common conception. At Sadguru, we believe that:

- Watershed development is not merely an activity, or a project to be taken up in isolation;
- Watershed approach is a comprehensive, holistic, multi-disciplinary and multi-sectorial concept;
- It encompasses several inter-related activities and interventions around land and water resources in the given area; and
- The total impact of all the activities taken up simultaneously exceeds the sum of the impacts of each of these activities taken up individually. In other words, there is synergy among all the activities and interventions prescribed under the approach.

Sadguru's Watershed Development Programme

Usually, in most of the cases, a watershed development programme is implemented without integration or without the convergence of all essential activities and soil and moisture conservation work predominates the programme. Other activities such as tree plantation, water harvesting through tiny check dams and gabions, development of common wastelands and animal husbandry receive very little attention. But in Sadguru's programmes, various land and water resources development activities are very well integrated with other activities. For example, there is a relatively high emphasis on water resources development and tree plantation activities along with soil and moisture conservation. As the amount allotted under the Government-sponsored watershed development projects is normally not adequate to develop water resources, Sadguru mobilizes additional funds from various sources including Government and ensures the integration and convergence of all inter-related activities to derive highest possible benefits from their synergy and to cover larger area and larger population. For example, in Sadguru's watershed development projects, if there is potential for constructing a relatively bigger check dam costing, say, about Rs. 20 lakh, the activity is taken up, mobilizing the additional resources from various agencies. This is done because the impounding of substantially higher volume of water in the bigger dam would produce higher net benefits to the village than the smaller one. Similarly, if there is scope for community lift irrigation scheme, it is also taken up irrespective of the amount of funds allocated by the government under watershed project. In almost all the watershed projects that Sadguru has taken up, such integration and convergence has taken place and on an average, Sadguru has raised almost double the amount allocated by the government for the project taken up. It is very rare, if not impossible, that such an effective integration and convergence and mobilization of resources to such a high extent take place elsewhere in India. In fact, the C. H. Hanumantha Rao Committee had clearly recommended that, if necessary, the Project Implementation Agency should mobilize more funds to integrate the activities, which cannot be managed with the funds allocated by the government. Sadguru has implemented this suggestion consistently in all its watershed projects. As expected, this approach has produced very good results and impacts. For example, besides harvesting of surface run off, the approach has led to substantial increase in the groundwater table in the watershed and there is no scarcity of drinking water even in worst drought years. This is because of recharge of water in a large number of wells in the project villages. Besides, due to this approach, substantial area has been brought under irrigation in project villages, increasing agricultural production and income and insulating the villages from the adverse effects of scanty rainfall, or droughts.

Sadguru's watershed programme is characterized by the following special features:

- **Relatively high contribution and participation by people**

In the Government watershed development programmes, beneficiaries have to contribute 10% of the cost of the programme. But in the Sadguru's projects, they willingly contribute 30% of the cost in kind (in the form of labour). The extent of their participation in the programme is also markedly higher than in government programmes.

➢ **Sustainability through institutional building**

Often the community level institutions built under watershed development programmes collapse soon after a project is completed. In Sadguru's watershed projects, there are activities such as community lift irrigation, community water harvesting structures, horticulture development and joint forest management, which continue even after the watershed project is over, and therefore, the village institutions built up around these activities continue and impart sustainability to the watershed projects. Even the Self-Help Groups (SHGs) in Sadguru's project villages are involved in some kind of economic activities and are also associated with community irrigation systems, community forest management, horticulture, vegetable cultivation, milk producing, etc. All those SHGs are strong and viable groups, rendering post project sustainability.

➢ **'Watershed Plus' activities**

When the first phase of watershed development programme was over, many people started talking about and advocating the need for a 'watershed plus' programme. Though many were not clear what they meant by 'watershed plus'. One commonly understood meaning of ' watershed plus, was to undertake certain activities which could not be taken up during the implementation phase of watershed projects due to various constraints including inadequate allocation of funds. In other words, some people were arguing for allocation of more funds for extension of the projects, and named this as 'watershed plus' activities. We in Sadguru always believe that all kinds of relevant and inter-related development activities should be taken up during the prime implementation period itself and for doing this, if necessary, additional funds should be mobilized. Sadguru has implemented this 'watershed plus' concept during the implementation phase of its projects. Therefore, Sadguru did not support the commonly used concept of 'watershed plus'. Having developed our own concept of 'watershed plus' we undertook several additional developmental activities in our watershed project villages during the post -project period, which could be described as 'watershed plus' activities. Of course, the foundation for such' watershed plus' activities was laid during the implementation phase itself. In many of the project villages, such activities included horticulture, floriculture, and dairying. Also, recharging of wells on a large scale was taken up during the post-project period. This ensured not only the provision of assured irrigation but also facilitated the undertaking of highly profitable activities like horticulture, floriculture, etc. Not in many places elsewhere in India, such 'watershed plus' activities have been taken up. In most of the projects, both the Project Implementation Agency (PIA) and users just do not know what to take up under 'watershed plus' activities. A lesson from Sadguru suggests that the foundation for such watershed plus activities has to be laid during the project implementation phase itself as far as possible.

➢ **In-House training facilities**

Sadguru had set up in 1995 a full-fledged training institute of its own. It is equipped with modern teaching aids and facilities. The Institute organizes 150 plus training courses every year for government functionaries and NGO personnel in various functional areas including watershed development. This enables the Sadguru staff to get the first hand knowledge about the various rural development programmes underway in India and problems encountered in their implementation. Besides, being a reputed NGO in the field of NRM, Sadguru attracts a large number of distinguished visitors from both India and abroad including watershed development professionals. Interactions of Sadguru staff with those professionals broaden their perspective and enhance their knowledge about various aspects of watershed development and management. This in turn leads to the improvement in the quality of our watershed projects.

Impact of Sadguru's Watershed Projects

The ex-post evaluation of a few of Sadguru's watershed development projects has been recently initiated. One such study was conducted in the Kalapipal watershed during the period, 2002-03. The Kalapipal watershed falls in the scarce rainfall zone in Jhalod taluka, Dahod district of Gujarat. The zone has an annual normal rainfall of 828 mm. In the pre-project stage, the watershed had vast chunks of degraded lands and used to face extreme scarcity of even drinking water. Large-scale seasonal migration of labour in search of employment was prevalent in the area. Rainfed cropping and wage labour were the major sources of income. The project was launched in 1996. The highlights of the ex-post evaluation case study are presented in Box 4.1:

Box 4.1 - The Economic Impact of Watershed Project

Increase in area under cultivation

The project efforts resulted in an average increase of 20 % in the area under cultivation. The extension of cultivated land was possible because of bringing the long fallow under plough.

Increase in Irrigation

The irrigation increased by 13 % from wells and taking into account, the community lift irrigation schemes, there was overall 38 % increase in irrigation in the watershed area which is significant.

Cropping intensity

The cropping intensity, which was 89 % in the pre-project stage, increased to 165 % in the post-project stage.

Changes in cropping pattern

Significant diversification in the cropping pattern was observed due to the project impact as the total number of crops under cultivation was only 6 during the pre-project stage, which increased to 9 in the post-project stage. Dry land horticultural crops like mango, Amla and lemon were introduced on a significant scale in the watershed area of horticulture.

Impact on Yield of crops

The yield of the main crop of maize in the watershed on the dry-land was comparable with that in irrigated maize indicating the improved moisture regime in the watershed. Significant increase in yield of all the crops was observed in the post project stage. For example, there was increase of 25% in maize ; about 33 % in pigeon pea and 140 % in wheat. The abnormal rise in the yields of the wheat could be attributed to the fact that prior to irrigation, they were raising non-irrigated wheat depending on the residue moisture of monsoon and with the availability of irrigation, apparently the yields increased manifolds.

Impact on Fodder Availability

The total production of fodder from different crops showed a minimum increase of 10.25 % (in case of Maize) to a maximum increase of 1372% (in case of Paddy). The sharp increase in paddy fodder was due to increase in area sown on account of watershed development.

The average per hectare increase in yield from different crops was recorded to be 154.19 % in kharif and the overall increase in the agriculture production in the entire watershed was 43.63 % in kharif.

During the Rabi season, the fodder yield from different crops showed an increase ranging from a minimum of 12.5 % (in case of Wheat) to a maximum of 100 % (in case of Gram). Similarly, the production of fodder from different crops ranged from a minimal increase of 197.27 % (in case of Gram) to a maximum of 576.93 % (in case of Wheat). The overall increase in the yield (q/ha) was reported to be about 22.22 % (exclusive of the yield from vegetables).

Impact on groundwater resources

The change in the ground water level was measured through the observatory wells in the watershed area over the period, 1997-2002. The maximum increase in the ground water level in the wells was recorded during the month of June 1999 and it was of the order of 2.72 meters.

It is important to know that even during the four consecutive years of drought from 1999-2002, the water level in the observatory wells has remained more or less constant or showed an increase. This can be concluded from the fact that there has been a considerable effect of the water harvesting measures, which led to the recharging of the ground water level, which in turn is reflected in the increased water levels, despite drought conditions.

Impact on allied activities

Next to farming, the dairy activity picked up in a substantial measure. The net income from dairy activity increased from Rs. 1.25 lakhs in the pre-project stage to Rs. 7.45 lakhs for the hamlet in the post-project stage. Due to increase in the assured fodder supply within the watershed and restriction imposed on free grazing on common lands, the stall-fed dairy activity developed rapidly from the earlier activity of sheep rearing.

Reduction in the extent of seasonal migration

Due to the increased availability of employment opportunities within the watershed, the seasonal migration was dramatically reduced. Employment in the farm sector increased substantially and the project work also provided ample employment to the landless. The incremental employment per hectare of GCA was 18 mandays per annum. The study revealed that the relative shares of different occupations within the watershed had undergone a significant change with new sources of income like fruits and vegetables crops.

Impact on social sector

The increase in income and the relative stability provided by watershed development had induced several positive impacts on education, housing, and health care. The enrolment of children in primary as well as secondary standards has gone up, while numbers of dropouts from the school have reduced substantially. There was an improvement in the ratio of girls to boys in school enrolment as also participation of elders in the non-formal education programme. About 35 % of the houses were either renovated or converted to pucca houses..

The above impact is from the rainfed conditions. In Sadguru's watershed projects, water resources development is a prominent feature carried out by mobilizing additional funds, and as a result, in most of the watershed projects of Sadguru, sizeable irrigation is developed, resulting in much greater impact, rather amazing impact, described in the chapter of Water Resources Development.

Some Lessons from Sadguru Experience

No generalizations about watershed development programmes in India can be made on the basis of Sadguru's experience and a single case study. However, the following lessons that seem to us to be useful for designing improved systems of watershed management can be drawn from our experiences:

Ensure transparency and accountability and proper utilization of public money

From our interactions with NGO personnel and government functionaries engaged in watershed development and management, it is evident that watershed development programmes in most of the states is not done faithfully and hence the intended benefits from them are not realized.

In the context of empowerment of people and their institutions, particularly PRIs, through devolution of financial powers, some people argue that such a step would empower the

PRIs and village community. If this were true, we as NGOs would be extremely happy as we also subscribe to the argument for real empowerment of PRIs. But, on ground, the situation is entirely different from the intentions. Transfer of funds to PRIs alone cannot bring about their empowerment. The empowerment would come if the funds transferred were utilized properly and good results were obtained. If the money is properly utilized and results are good, it builds the confidence among people for handling successfully such funds and this confidence and improved living condition on account of successful implementation of development projects brings real empowerment.

Select a competent Project Implementing Agency (PIA)

This is a basic pre-requisite for success of any watershed development project. The selection of PIA must be made on the basis of merit alone, as judged by the technical and professional competence and credibility based on past performance. This criterion must be adhered to ruthlessly irrespective of type of PIA under consideration. All prospective PIAs, whether Panchayati Raj Institutions (PRIs), Government Departments, or NGOs, must be evaluated using this criterion, whosoever is found most competent and capable should be entrusted with the responsibility of implementation of the project. No other criteria would deliver the desired results. If results of the project are good and people are satisfied, the politicians can easily take the credit for the success and improve their hold on the people and garner more votes. Sooner our politicians, across the party lines, understand this basic logic, better it will be for them.

Provide flexibility in guidelines for implementation

The guidelines issued by the Ministry of Rural Development are very rigid. Despite the appreciation of the role of NGOs in rural development by the Prime Minister, Chief Ministers and many other dignitaries on all platforms, the policy makers do not take cognizance of their critical role while framing the guidelines. Two examples may suffice to substantiate my argument. One, the SGSY Special Project guidelines issued by the Government of India,

Department of Rural Development allow the cooperatives, industries, and international organizations to implement this programme, but the NGOs are excluded for the reasons best known to those who framed the guidelines. This is an absurd policy. The international organizations usually do not implement the programmes, but they are included. The industries are considered appropriate to implement but not the NGOs, even those with proven track record. Two, the newly launched Hariyali scheme of the Government of India also does not provide for, in its guidelines, the involvement of NGOs in implementing the programme. In the guidelines of Hariyali scheme, the NGOs are to be selected as the last option when no other PIAs, i.e., PRIs, Government Departments, and universities, are found suitable or are available. The guideline in Item 12 specifies a criterion for selection of NGOs as PIA, but stops short of stipulating that wherever right kind of NGOs are available, they should be involved. The intention of Guideline in Item 12 is further diluted, if not contradicted, by the omission of any reference to the role of NGOs, in the Foreword and the Preface to the Hariyali Guidelines written by the Secretary, Rural Development, and Additional Secretary, Rural Development, respectively. As a result of this, many State Governments (almost all state governments) are not going to involve NGOs in the implementation of the Hariyali scheme. This is a glaring omission. The state like Gujarat which has involved NGOs in almost all fields, is also, under above Hariyali guideline, side lining NGOs. As per our information the only state government which has refused to implement the above guidelines is Orissa, telling that they would not necessarily and exclusively involve PRIs in implementation of Hariyali scheme.

When it comes to the implementation of economic development programme, the first and foremost criteria should be the competency of the implementing agency. Unfortunately, in our country, the ruling elite think that the government money is their own money and they have a right to waste it under the garb of PRIs.

The way out for the better result of such economic

development programme is to entrust the implementation to the right agency. It could be PRIs, it could be government departments, or it could be NGOs. Whoever is more competent and more equipped to deliver the good in the given district or given tehsil, need to be entrusted the implementation.

Remove ambiguities and ensure uniform interpretation of guidelines

Whereas flexibility is a desirable feature, there should not be any ambiguities in the guidelines, particularly in matters relating to the roles and responsibilities of various stakeholders involved. I would like to cite here an example of how the same (watershed development) guidelines issued by the Union Ministry of Rural development in 2001 were interpreted differently by two State governments while allocating responsibility for implementation of watershed development projects. The guidelines stipulate that the highest priority in assigning the responsibility for implementation of watershed projects should be given to PRIs, followed by the Government departments and NGOs. This is mentioned in Clause 27 of the Guidelines. This clause does not exclude NGOs. In fact, in the following clause (28) of the same Guidelines, certain criteria are specified for selection of NGOs as PIAs. Using its own interpretation of Clause 27, the Rajasthan government, I understand its cabinet, decided to entrust the implementation of all the watershed projects to PRIs, excluding NGOs altogether. It would be heartening if the Government of Rajasthan sponsors an independent reputed organization to find out as to how the PRIs in Rajasthan have fared in the implementation of such a crucial programme.

While Rajasthan Government has interpreted and implemented the above guidelines as per their convenience and discretion, the same guidelines were interpreted and implemented by the Government of Gujarat very differently. Whereas, in the second phase of watershed development programme starting from 2000, the Rajasthan government has not allotted any watershed projects to NGOs, the Gujarat state has allotted as high a share as 83 % of the projects to the NGOs. We all know Gujarat is a cradle of NGOs. It is the land of Mahatma Gandhi, Sardar Vallabhbhai Patel, Ravishanker Maharaj, and many other great leaders and visionaries, who were responsible for setting up a number of reputed NGOs, before and after independence. This precious legacy is kept intact by many NGOs in Gujarat even today.

Avoid contradictions in policies and programmes of different government agencies

Besides ambiguities, another characteristic feature of the Government policies and programmes is the contradiction between objectives of programmes formulated by various departments. This is due mainly to the lack of inter-departmental coordination and cooperation. There are umpteen cases where such contradictions abound. Needless to emphasize, such contradictions are counter-productive. I foresee a possible solution to this problem. Recently, the Central Planning Commission has created a special Joint Machinery for Collaborative Relationship between the Government and the Voluntary Sector. In my opinion, under the auspices of this Machinery, the Planning Commission could play an important role in identifying and removing such contradictions and ensure the adoption of an integrated and coordinated approach to resolve rural development problems that cut across several departments / ministries of the Central and State governments. However, with the change in government in New Delhi in the middle of May 2004, we do not know the fate of above Joint Machinery and the process started by outgoing Planning Commission of Government of India for adopting policy framework for the involvement of NGOs in the government programmes.

Avoid putting "Old Wine in a New Bottle"

We as a nation have witnessed many rural development schemes that were renamed or replaced by new ones, a few years after their launching. Some of the schemes are replaced after five years and lucky ones last ten years. When we look into the ingredients, components and objectives of the old and new schemes, we find that they were more or less similar in their design and objectives and then wonder why they were replaced by new ones. Now it is widely accepted that the main reason for failures of our rural development schemes or any other schemes was the poor implementation. Therefore, what was needed was the improved implementation with some changes in the design and instruments of the same schemes instead of replacing them by new schemes. Instead of taking remedial measures to improve the implementation and curb the mal-practices in the implementation, the Government found it more expedient to replace the schemes by their new avtars.

A perusal of the components of the Hariyali scheme would reveal that there is hardly anything new in the scheme except that its name is different. When the announcement of Hariyali scheme was made by the Prime Minister, the impression was that it was going to be a new and additional scheme of rural development. Now that we have in our hand the guidelines, it is clear that it is not a new programme. It is only a new name of an old scheme, formulated by merging the watershed development programme of the Union Ministry of Rural Development.

The Hariyali scheme is, however, different from the earlier on in terms of administrative structure at the village level. In the new scheme, the gram sabha will be treated as a watershed association, the village panchayat will perform the functions of the erstwhile watershed committee (WC) and the sarpanch of the village panchayat will serve as Chairman and the Patwari will be the secretary of the WC. It is alright to entrust to the gram sabha the role of watershed association, but making village panchayats as WC is a dangerous ploy and still worse is the proposal to make sarpanch the chairman and patwari the secretary of WC, giving them powers to operate the accounts. There are better and more democratic ways to administer the scheme at the village level. For example, the gram sabha could be allowed to elect a watershed committee and the watershed committee, in turn, could elect a chairman and appoint a secretary, who is accountable to the WC through the elected chairman. Any educated person in the village or a nearby village can be appointed as secretary either by the gram sabha or the WC. This change is essential if we want to reduce the risk involved in handling huge sums of public funds at the village level. In a nutshell, I would like to emphasize the need for taking all possible safe guards to prevent possible embezzlement of the funds and grants and the consequent failure of the Scheme. If large numbers of PRIs fail, in implementing this scheme properly and thereby the scheme fails in benefiting the community the framers of guidelines and those involved in implementation, supervising and monitoring must be held responsible for such failures. If Government is keen to ensure the success of Hariyali scheme, it must do couple of minimum things. Entrust project to a competent agency from any sector, PRI, the Department or NGOs, whoever is competent in the given area. When entrusted to the PRIs, they should be encouraged to take services of the competent department or competent NGO to ensure technical soundness of the project. I would also like to draw attention to certain potential, but, serious problems in implementation of Hariyali guidelines in its present shape. How will we deal with group gram panchayats where watershed project area may be in one village and the Gram Panchayat Sarpanch may be from other village? How shall we resolve this situation as in such case the Sarpanch may not have a stake in the watershed programme? How about the Gram Panchayat is superseded on some reasons by the Government ? Also, though Sarpanch may be elected, but, he may be elected by a minority votes with majority of the votes going to the rival candidates. In this situation, Sarpanch may not be enjoying confidence of the entire village. The best option is to appoint Chairman of watershed committee from among the users group. This is much more democratic for the specific programme than what is provided in the guidelines.

It is now two years since the Hariyali scheme was launched in April 2003. All the apprehensions expressed by many on Hariyali Guidelines are now coming true. The scheme has hardly taken of at most of the places. It is in real 'mess'. PRIs are not equipped. No full time qualified WDT available at most of the places, no motivation and enthusiasm among PRIs and Government on this scheme. If two years experience is of any indication, scheme is destined to fail, unless Guidelines is modified and better implementation arrangements are ensured. Summary of feed back from several districts offers following state of affairs of Hariyali scheme.

The Feedback and Informations from the field on Hariyali Scheme

We have interacted very actively with large numbers of watershed developed team members of 8 districts on Hariyali scheme and common observations received were as follows ;

- Even after nearly two years of its implementation, Haryali scheme has hardly taken off.
- Most of the watershed development teams are lacking any experience in watershed development.
- Almost all the WDT members have been chosen from the regular staff of block / tehsil panchayats and they have to carry out both their main functions and in addition they have to carry out watershed development works.
- Almost all the WDT members expressed that they cannot give justice to their both functions, i.e. regular functions and that of watershed work.
- In many cases the transfer of WDT members is reported which affects result in the implementation.
- Not a single WDT member reported that he was happy with his association with Hariyali scheme. On the contrary almost all of them said they were not likely to succeed.
- Most of the WDT members reported that Panchayats being an elected body, it was difficult to deal with them in the implementation of this kind of programme.

People completed this massive water harvesting structure in 85 days, indicating their interest, involvement & ownership.

Before construction in month of November-December.

Jhalawar villagers dicussing water distribution issues

The Joint Secretary, Ministry of Tribal Affairs, Government of India, Commissioner Tribal Development, Gujarat and Project Administrator, Dahod on a visit to our Institute.

Women members of the Horticulture co-operatives and groups in their Annual General Meeting.

Well fully recharged after recharging technique under watershed development

Principal Secretary, Rural Development, Rajasthan, along with Directors of DRDAs in Rajasthan on field visit in our watershed activities.

Opening welcome note by Mr. Harnath Jagawat at the Silver Jublee Celebration of the organisation

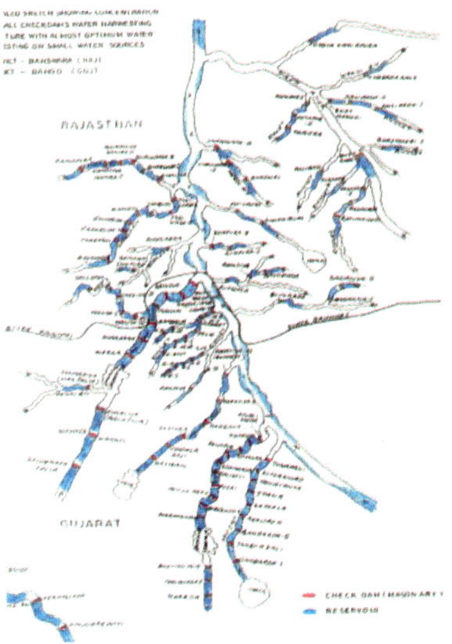

Strategy of Revival of Rivers promoted by the organisation since the beginning.

Women managed drinking water system installed in partnership by the co-operative and federation

Common Waterland developed into an Horticulture Orchard by the village irrigation Co-operative & Federation

The forest raised by the tribal communities under the joint forest management and treated land under watershed on the foothill

Tribal women handling drip irrigation system in her horticulture orchard

Standing Bumper crop of Summer Groundnut in Mota Dharola L I Scheme.
The annual earning in the scheme has increased from
Rs. 12 lakhs to Rs. 1.4 crores.

A newly constructed Community Lift Irrigation Scheme at village Varod is a Specimen of the quality of workmanship of Sadguru

Wheat field under the Community Lift Irrigation in Jhalawar, Rajasthan

CHAPTER - 5

Land-Based Income Generating Activities

In Chapters 2 and 3, I discussed two of Sadguru's major interventions, namely, water resources development and management and watershed development and management. These two interventions were primarily aimed at restoration and improvement in the land and water resources of the project area. Land and water are two of critical natural resources that determine the level and pace of agricultural development. Their development, conservation and optimum utilization is necessary for sustainable agricultural development. Keeping in view it's mission of improving the quality of life of people in its project area, which depends, to a large extent, on per capita income, Sadguru thought it necessary at the outset to promote existing and introduce new land-based income generating activities in its project area. So naturally, agriculture, horticulture and agro-forestry emerged as the high priority areas for its initial interventions. In this chapter, I describe and discuss the major activities of Sadguru in these three areas and their impacts.

Agriculture

The condition of agriculture and horticulture in the tribal regions, particularly in the semi-arid regions has been far from satisfactory due to several reasons including a fragile natural resource base. Agriculture in the tribal region is characterized by low and fluctuating crop yields, and low level of input use. Unlike other farmers in our country, the tribals are not traditionally a farming community. It was only after the nationalization of forests in India that the farming became a prime source of their livelihood; prior to that they depended almost wholly on forests for their livelihood. Thus, the farming history of the tribals is very recent, unlike other farmers in India who have a history of nearly 5,000 years of agriculture. Besides, the recent entry of the tribals in agriculture, another constraint in the development of good agriculture was the lack of irrigation development in most of our tribal regions. This in conjunction with extremely small holdings of poor quality land and recurrent droughts rendered agriculture in the tribal regions financially non-viable. Hence they did not have high stakes in agriculture as a means of their livelihood and did not put in their best efforts and required inputs in it.

In view of the above status and context of tribal agriculture, and as mentioned in Chapters 1 and 2, Sadguru used water as an entry point in its project villages. It constructed check dams for impounding rain water, installed lift irrigation systems, and undertook activities for recharging of groundwater and introduced high value crops to enable the farmers to make more profitable use of water. The availability of irrigation made good impact on the agriculture in the project villages.

With their own experience during their migration to agriculturally progressive regions in Gujarat and other adjoining areas, where they worked as labourers on the farm of progressive farmers and with the extension services provided by Sadguru, the tribals picked up irrigated farming fairly well. Their crop yields have increased at least 4-5 times with one additional cropping season and under perennial irrigation, the yields have increased about nine times. The availability of irrigation has also helped them to go in for new and more profitable cropping pattern, including shift to vegetable cultivation, which on a small patch would fetch them very good income. Thousands of tribal farmers in the project area have now taken to more profitable cropping patterns. This is a real transformation of tribal agriculture, thanks to the availability of water. The scale at which water resources have been developed under Sadguru's programmes is quite big; irrigation facilities have developed for 93,931 acres of the overall command and about 187862 acres of cropped area benefiting more than 51219 tribal / rural households.

As narrated in preceding para, when tribal farmers get irrigation, their yields and income increase by five times and when they get perennial irrigation, their yields and income go by about nine times. These are the facts collected from several years of experiences, substantiated by large numbers of studies.

Horticulture

With small holdings, limited availability of irrigation and plenty of labour, cultivation of high value horticultural crops such as fruits and vegetables is a better option than maize and jowar for the farming community in the region. Keeping this in view, Sadguru recently introduced horticulture in its project villages. It has since been picking up very fast. Once the farmers got good returns from their irrigated crops, they acquired confidence in their farming operations and were willing to go for better options that became available with the introduction of irrigation and extension services of sadguru. More than 13,962 plots of equal numbers of farmers had been developed by the tribals under the horticultural development programme by the end of December 2004. Based on this encouraging response from tribals, we in sadguru are now envisaging that every year around 3,000 or more plots of equal numbers of farmers would be brought under this programme.

In this programme, one plot measuring about half an acre of the land is taken up. On average, each plot has the potential of generating as high net income as Rs. 40,000 per annum from the horticultural crops selected for this programme. I would like to mention in this context that the introduction of high value horticultural crops has been accompanied by adoption of the most advanced technology of drip and sprinkler systems of micro irrigation. These two interventions have resulted in more efficient use of scarce water resources, increased yields and higher incomes. Hundreds of such micro irrigation systems have been put up on the horticulture plots of tribal farmers in our project area. Another interesting feature of this sophisticated advanced technology is that it is managed by the tribal women after some training imparted by Sadguru.

Now, soon after its introduction, this technology of drip and sprinkler systems has been mastered by the apex irrigation federation of our tribal farmers and the tribal boys have become experts in the installation of these systems. They have perfected the skill so much that the premier manufacturing company of this system, Jain Irrigation System, has given a certificate to the federation and the tribal boys that they are the best in such installation work.

Side by side with the cultivation of vegetables, in several villages, floriculture has been developed on small patches of land (one fifth or one fourth of an acre). Consequently, tribal farmers, who have taken to floriculture, are earning Rs. 150-500 per day from the sale of flowers. The floriculture plots have drip irrigation systems. A success story of a village, Rozam, which may be called the first floriculture village of Dahod district, is presented in Box 5.1 below.

Box - 5.1

Rozam, a small village in Dahod taluka with 100 % tribal population, which is 12 kilometers away from Dahod district headquarter, is a live example of success of floriculture. It was the hard work of the villagers that gave a good shape to the programme of floriculture. The villagers earlier cultivated cereal crops like maize, toor, etc. but, since 2001 started floricultural practices and the benefits were many.

Ramilaben Rathod, along with other villagers were taken on exposure visit to Southern and Western Gujarat (Junagadh, Valsad, Navsari, Anand, Jalgaon, etc.). Training was also imparted to them to motivate them for horticulture plantation. In first year of the programme, she received grafted plants from the organization and cultivated the crops in just 0.20 hectare of her total land area. After seeing the profit, she increased the area and is presently cultivating even vegetables in 0.12 hectares of her total land area.

During the interval of horticulture crop plantation, Ramilaben started floriculture practices. In the first year, she cultivated Rose in 0.08 hectare and Marigold in 0.05 hectares. The profit from this was very high. She sold Roses worth Rs. 55,000/- in nine months and Marigold worth Rs. 10,400/- in three months. In one year, she earned Rs. 65,400/- a profit which motivated her to further this practice. A year later, Ramilaben made a nursery of 2,000 plants by grafting the mother plants and sold them at the rate of Rs. 5/- per plant. She earned a profit of Rs. 10,000/- just from the flower plants.

In Rozam today, tribal women have opted for more than 250 fruit orchards and more than 300 floriculture plots, large number of them inter-cropping with horticulture. Even with the nominal price, their earnings are at par with the farmers of the progressive areas with large number of farmers earning Rs. 150/- to Rs. 300/- every day by selling flowers. On festival days, the earnings are much more as the prices are much more.

It is rightly said that "there is only one magic on this planet and it is contained in water". The story of Rozam village testifies this dictum. As one could see in Box 5.2 as also in chapters of this book, water has created a magical impact on the livelihoods of tribals. These developments in horticulture including floriculture in project area have great potential and great hope for the poor tribals all over the country.

Forestry-related Activities

Before I discuss Sadguru's interventions in the forestry sector, I would like to digress a bit and present the past and present scenarios of forests in the country in general and Dahod district in particular. This would serve as a good background for assessing the relevance of our activities in this sector.

Past Scenario in India and Dahod

Forests and the tribals are inseparable from each other. In India, most of the tribal habitations are adjacent to forest lands. In other words, virtually in most of the tribal villages and each of the tribal districts, large chunks of forest land exist. It is estimated that nearly 29% of the total geographical area of all the tribal districts is classified as forest lands. Another about 25 % or more of the non-forest land in these districts like wastelands, culturable waste, and grazing lands gaucher are degraded and undulating and hence more suitable for forestry than agriculture. Thus, we could say that, on average, a typical tribal district in India has nearly 50 % of its land, which has high potential for forestry. Such lands belong to the state Forest and Revenue Departments, concerned village panchayats, other village organizations, and individuals. But all such lands are indeed a very valuable asset in the tribal areas.

But sadly, the tribals have got a raw deal from all other sections of our society. First, the invaders pushed them into the remote hills and forests. Then, the need and greed of the Britishers played havoc on the tribals. The nationalization of the forests under the Forest Act of 1864 and stringent provisions in the subsequent Forest Act dispossessed tribals of their own forest land and this draconian Act gave the biggest blow to the tribals and their economy as till then the tribals depended almost fully on the forests and forest products for their livelihood. In the recent history, no other community has been deprived of its main source of income to this extent and magnitude. More sadly, the gross injustice and consequent deprivation caused by the British Government's action has not been remedied by our own Government. On the contrary, our own government has further deprived the tribals of their inherent rights on the forests. In particular, indiscriminate implementation of the Forest Conservation Act of 1980 has in many cases deprived the tribals of their access to water, roads, electricity, etc. I have digressed to bring home a serious point that the miseries of tribals started from taking away forests from them and depriving them of their basic rights to livelihood.

Present Scenario in Dahod

Now, I will briefly describe the status of forests in Dahod district, where Sadguru launched its activities initially. Like all the tribal regions in our country, this district also had vast chunks of forest lands, accounting for nearly 75 % of its total geographical area about 100 years ago. But over a time, the forest land in Dahod district has been drastically reduced and now forms only about 25 % of its total geographical area. Stories of thick and dense forests in the district about 100 years back, as told by elderly men and women, abound. The district gazetteer also corroborates such stories. I myself recall travelling by rail and road through the dense and thick forests in the area 40-50 years back.

Against this backdrop, what we see in the district in the name of forests is distressing. Though as per the Government records, even today 25 % of the total geographical area of the district is under 'reserved forests', our general observations corroborated by the Remote Sensing Imageries present a dismal picture of the forest areas in the district. Most of the forest areas are deforested and land degraded. The survival of new plantations by the Forest Department is satisfactory up to 3-5 years. Things have degenerated to such a level that in many so called forests areas, one cannot see a single tree for miles together. Unless drastic steps are taken by the government to arrest this trend and restore the degraded forests, a substantial chunk of land in the district will soon become arid from the present status of semi-arid. In a recent celebration of the World Environment Day in Dahod district on 5th June 2003, the Conservator of Forests, Vadodara Circle, himself described that part of the area in the district was heading towards desertification.

Who should intervene and how

It is now commonly agreed that in the tribal areas of Dahod district, most of the land is more suitable for the forestry than agriculture. About 25 % of the land owned by people is more suitable for tree plantation than crop cultivation. Another about 25 % of the land is owned by the Forest Department itself and is meant for forestry. Thus, roughly about 50 %, or about 2,95,000 hectares, of the land in the tribal areas of the district are more suitable for forestry or tree plantation. Imagine the impact of tree plantation on such a massive scale on the economy, environment and livelihoods of local tribals in the district. This high potential offers a real challenge to the Government, NGOs and people. Similar potential exists in other tribal districts such as Jhabua in MP and Banswara in Rajasthan and in all tribal regions throughout the country.

Who can accomplish this massive task on which the entire future of this tribal region depends? With due respect and apology to some honest and sincere forests officials, I would like to assert that it is now certain that the Forest Department alone cannot restore the forests in the district. Extreme poverty of local people, particularly, those living close to the forests, compounded by the existence of mafia / gangs of unscrupulous traders masterminding large scale illicit cuttings and enjoying the patronage and protection of politicians, will not allow the best of the forest officials to succeed in restoring the forests in the district. In last about 30 years or so, the strength of forest staff in the district has increased by four times, but, ironically, the population of grown up forest trees has gone down very much of the level 30-40 years ago. Thus, there is no possibility of improvement in this situation notwithstanding the latest forest conservation Act, as the forces engaged in deforestation are stronger than the Forest Department.

The only other alternative to ensure success in the restoration of forests is to entrust the afforestation work to the tribals themselves, by leasing out the forest land to them for raising the forests. The Forest Department should supply the inputs and monitor strictly that only trees are raised on such forest land leased out to the tribals or their community institutions. There is 86,149 hectares of forest land in the tribal areas of Dahod district. At the rate of one hectare of forest land leased to one family, nearly 86,000 families can be involved in this programme. This would provide massive employment opportunities to the poor tribals and at the same time help in regenerating forests under various Government programmes and ensure the restoration of degraded forests. Along with the afforestation of the forest land on above lines, tree plantation on private land that are more suitable for forestry has also to be encouraged. There is potential for raising forestry on nearly 2,00,000 hectares of privately owned land in the tribal areas of the district. The Joint Forest Management programme, if implemented sincerely and honestly, could be helpful in the development and protection of forests in the district.

Now, I will briefly describe the major interventions made by Sadguru in the forestry sector and their impacts.

Agro-Forestry and Farm Forestry

Based on the past history and potential of forests in the district as presented above and keeping in view the need for appropriate land use practices, Sadguru attached high importance to the forestry programme from the beginning. Since it was not possible at that time to work on the forest land, the approach adopted by the organization was to develop forestry on the private land suitable for the plantation and some other land under the agro forestry and farm forestry pattern. Year after year a massive programme of tree plantation has been taken up since 1982. About 50,000 acres has been brought under the agro-forestry and farm forestry programme by Sadguru Foundation covering about 56,000 tribal households, mainly in Dahod district of Gujarat and to some extent in Banswara district of Rajasthan.

The experience of forestry on private wastelands in the tribal areas of the district under the agro forestry and farm forestry pattern has been very encouraging. The tribals have fully realized that once they have few trees of their own, they would be able to cope with the problems created by recurrent droughts. Irrigation may fail them, but not the trees in the years of droughts. This is amply demonstrated in many cases, in which each family sold trees worth Rs. 5,000 to Rs. 15,000 in a drought year and sustained their livelihood.

Thus trees are serving as non-formal insurance against exigencies. The owning of trees make them feel secured and confident in facing the calamities like droughts. There are large numbers of villages in Dahod district each having tree wealth worth lakhs of rupees. In fact, there are large numbers of individual households each owning trees worth Rs. 1-2 lakhs. This programme has been replicated in more than 450 villages in the Sadguru's project area because the tribals responded very well to this programme.

Though often tribals have sold their trees in the years of droughts to meet their household needs, we had interesting observations in some of the villages. In one of our studies, we came to know from a sample of villagers that instead of cutting and selling their trees in the drought year, they sell their animals and / or ornaments or borrow money. The reason given for this behaviour was that the value of tree would appreciate sharply in the next few years while the value of the animals or ornaments was not going to increase that sharply. A wise decision and sound practice based on economics, indeed.

If and when a massive movement of tree plantation is initiated and the restoration of degraded forests is achieved, even if partially, it opens up the process of further development based on the forests and forest products and revolutionizes the economy of the region. One can dream of each tribal district in our country becoming a mini Sweden in developing forest based economy in not so remote a future, provided, of course, the policy makers and people take this potential seriously and harness it. Ignoring this potential and not taking any concrete action to harness it will cost people and area very heavily. Infact, it has already costed heavily to the community and nation as a whole.

Impact of Forestry Programme

The overall impact of Sadguru's forestry sector programmes, agro-forestry and farm forestry could be summarized as follows:

- The plantation has been done on about 50,000 acres of the land.
- More than 115 villages in the region have achieved tree cover on about 30-35% of the land in each village against almost no tree cover before the programme.
- All the beneficiaries of this programme numbering about 56,000 families have become self-sufficient in their fuel wood and timber wood requirements.
- The tree cover and owning of trees by tribal people has served as an insurance against exigencies such as droughts, or any other social difficulty situations as revealed by several studies.
- The massive plantation in every village has resulted in the

improvement in the micro environment and the eco-system.

- Sadguru's plantation villages are easily identifiable because of their massive tree cover.

- The availability of enough timber has improved the housing condition in the villages. In some old project villages, almost all the houses have been either renovated or newly constructed with the wood available from their own wood lots.

- As per our assessment, people must have used their own wood worth about more than Rs. 40 million in the construction of their houses.

- It is estimated that the trees worth about Rs. 3,000 millions (Rs. 300 crores) are in the possession of people in our project area. This is very conservative estimate.

- A unique feature of Sadguru's forestry programme is that it is totally and exclusively managed by women.

A success story is presented in Box – 5.2;

Box 5.2 - Development through Farm Forestry Development

Dhankiya Falia is a hamlet of village Zaribuzarg in Dahod Taluka. The hamlet has 60 households which were all migrating earlier. Due to the technical constraints, this hamlet was left out from the command of the community lift irrigation system installed in the village. With a view to bring the inhabitants of this hamlet on par with the beneficiaries of the community irrigation system, Sadguru staff motivated the dwellers of this hamlet to undertake recharging of their almost defunct wells in sizeable numbers and to undertake tree plantation on their field bunds and wastelands. Consequently, in 1988, a massive agro-forestry programme was introduced in this hamlet with the participation of the community. Each and every household planted a good number of trees the very first year of the programme.

In the year 1996, when an impact study of the above programme was conducted, the following amazing results were revealed :

- *At the end of 8 years of the programme in 1996, there were 2,000 - to 5,000 trees per family.*
- *All the wells that had been fully recharged were under active use and providing irrigation in 2-3 seasons every year.*
- *Nearly 70% of the households had constructed new houses using wood / timber from their own woodlot and the rest had renovated their houses from their own wood. Thus 100% households had used their own wood in the construction of new houses or renovation of old houses.*
- *Each of the house-hold had sold trees worth Rs. 2,000 - Rs. 20,000. This was in addition to the income from the agriculture in non-irrigated and irrigated land.*
- *With the revival of the eco-system, the hamlet has got a complete new look and is taking full benefits of the renewed resources such as water and trees made available through their efforts.*

Joint Forest Management

In 1992, the Government of India introduced a programme called Joint Forest Management (JFM). In this programme, local community is allotted a patch of degraded forest land for regeneration, conservation and protection. It is jointly implemented by the Forest Department and the community under the banner of a village forest protection committee. In some cases, NGOs are also partners in this programme.

Though Sadguru has developed forestry mainly on private lands under its agro- forestry and farm forestry activities, as described in the preceding section of this chapter, the organization has also initiated JFM programme in a few of its project villages. There are now 27 villages covered under JFM programme, where Sadguru is one of the partners along with the local community and the Forest Department. By and large, the JFM programme has progressed satisfactorily, but there have been a few set backs which prompted the organization not to expand this programme on a larger scale. One of the major difficulties has been the lack of adequate support and cooperation of the Forest Department, particularly, at the lower level or field level. In Gujarat and perhaps elsewhere, the Forest Department is keen to expand JFM programme for one reason or other, but, by and large, it is not keen on partnership with NGOs.

When we talk of the JFM programme, we believe that the success of the programme depends, to a large extent, on the DFO. Surprisingly, in our JFM programme in Banswara, Rajasthan, everything has been going well for last 8-9 years without any major problem. Two DFOs, from this region, have supported the programme which pleasantly surprised us, as we were expecting problems in Rajasthan.

However, the JFM programme is still in its infancy. Right now, the villagers are getting benefits from minor forest produce. The real test of the programme will be when the harvesting of final produce (timber) will take place. There is a lot of uncertainty about the condition of the forest under JFM 10 or 15 years from now, about the attitude of the Forest Department officials, and about the terms and conditions of sharing the benefits between the Forest department and village community. There is no consensus at the national level as to the ratio of sharing the ultimate benefits. In some states, 80 % of the benefits are to go to the community ; In some states 50 %. There is, thus, a great variation in the terms of sharing the ultimate benefits. There is also no scheme or provision for the forest related development activities in the JFM area. Besides, there are so many other issues that need to be resolved if this programme is to succeed. We are convinced that if this programme is managed well by all the partners, there is hope for the revival and survival of our forests and with that revival of tribal economy to a great extent.

Problem resolution in innovative ways

How a well meaning and essential Act is wrongly interpreted and badly implemented can be seen from the implementation of the Forest Conservation Act 1980. This Act was necessary, but need not be implemented in a manner that virtually harasses the local tribal community living in the vicinity of forests. Though there are several examples of the above Act not being implemented properly, I give an example of an incident we came across. The whole episode was included in the organization's Annual Report for the year 1996-97, and is reproduced below:

Box 5.3 - The Law that Denies Water to the Tribal Community

Reading the above title of this story, one may raise an immediate question, "Can there be any law that denies and deprives the community, access to the basic life need such as water?" Yes, there is such a law in the Republic of India. If that community is unfortunate to be in the neighborhood of the forest area or it is surrounded by the forest area, and if water is to be carried through the forest area. The Forest Conservation Act and the manner of its inhumane implementation, can certainly deny that water to the neighbourly community. "Love thy neighbour". Help your neighbour, "are the gospels not usually followed by the Forest Department, particularly, in implementing the above Conservation Act. How can any community cooperate with the Department which denies them the basic life needs?

Here is a concrete example (One of the several to be found in our country). Chhayan Kalapipal is 100 % tribal village in Tehsil Jhalod, District Panchmahals, Gujarat, where the State Tribal Development Department in collaboration with our Organization has installed a community lift irrigation scheme to meet the drinking water and irrigation needs of the above tribal village. The water source, a good tank, belongs to the community, but, to take water to the village and fields, the under ground pipe line of 8 inches diameter is to be laid through the length of only 400 meters forest area, where there are no trees and no land is to be lost by the Department, as the pipe line will be refilled by the soil and that small portion of the land will be brought to its original shape allowing the plantation to be raised. The Forest Department has disallowed laying of the pipe line under the above Act. There is a provision of the permission, and accordingly, the community through the local Tribal Development Office applied for permission in April 1996 and also made several representations to the Forest Department. The permission should have been promptly granted as the above work was not in any way detrimental to Forest Conservation. Yet, it has not been granted for one full year till the end of March 1997. Besides denial of drinking water, the poor tribal community has been deprived of irrigation in 225 acres of the land and as the farmers have lost two seasons of irrigation by March 1997, they have been deprived of the crop worth about Rs. 25 lacs. Who will compensate this loss? Does it not amount to a gross negligence in withholding such simple permission for one whole year, which was resulted in such huge loss to the tribal community?

If it was Hazira-Bijapur-Jagdishpur Gas pipeline of 1,400 kilometers, passing through the vast forest areas, with the constant width of more than 10 meters throughout such long distance, the summary permission would be issued by special ordinances. If it was a drinking water pipe line for the cities prompt permission would be granted, as the cities are powerful with strong political backing, which can prevail upon the Government for any work. But, when it comes to the poor tribal community, they are to be denied the basic right on crucial resources such as water, or they have to wait for years for the permission.

It is the case of Public Interest Litigation.

Where are our Human Rights Activists? Lost in Kashmir? Too busy in the Narmada water dispute? Or, why fight for a small cause, which may not give them International popularity? It is not a small issue. The sum total of such small issues spread over in the country's tribal regions makes it a big issue, worth making it a National and International issue.

Where are our otherwise pro-people courts? Our High Court or the Supreme Court should take serious note of such inhuman and insensitive implementation of the Statute and give justice to the tribal community in all such cases of the denials of basic life needs. The Statute should be suitably amended, making it obligatory for automatic permission within 3 months of the application, when the forest plantation will not be damaged or forest land will not be lost. May be it should be amended to the effect that none of the provisions of the above Act will deny the local community access to the water, electricity and the small village approach road, which may not be detrimental to the Forest Conservation.

The Gujarat Government's Department of Water Resources have evolved the most progressive policy in giving blanket permission to the tribal community for lifting water from reservoirs and canals situated in the tribal regions. Why the same policy cannot be adopted by the State Forest Department or the Central Government for giving blanket permission for the water, electricity, etc. in the forest regions, when such permission will not be detrimental to the Forest Conservation.

The spirit of the Forest Conservation Act is to conserve the forest and not the denial of the basic needs to the community in the vicinity of the forest area. To achieve best of the conservation with the least harassment to the community should be the implementation strategy of the Forest Department.

Having read above story in our above Annual Report, Mr. N. C. Saxena, who was then Secretary, Rural Development, Government of India, wrote on his own initiative a letter to the Chief Secretary, Government of Gujarat and the Secretary, Ministry of Environment and Forests, Government of India, stating that in his opinion, the provisions of Forest Conservation Act were not attracted in above situation and that the Forest Department should have taken more sympathetic view in the matter. As one of the most dynamic, most pragmatic and most people-oriented civil servant, Mr. Saxena on his own sought the interventions of the above high level officers in the matter.

Subsequently, the issue was settled, but, it took more than two years.

I think, the Forest Department in implementation of above Act should be careful that the local communities are not deprived of the right to meet their basic needs. If such rights are denied to them, they will not support the forest conservation and may, in fact, destroy the forest in vengeance.

There are many interesting incidents in which the local communities involved have resolved issues in amicable ways. I would cite one instance here. In one of our project villages, we got the permission from the Forest Department for installation of a pump house on a river bank which was in the forest jurisdiction. The permission for laying the underground pipe line for irrigation passing through the forest was also obtained. When the work was over and the pumps were to be operated by the villagers, they wanted to go to the pump house passing through the forest. Interestingly, the forest official stopped the villagers from going to the pump house, saying that the permission for the construction of the pump house was granted by the Department, but, there was no permission granted to them to pass through the forest to go to the pump house. The villagers were really stunned with this attitude of the forester. However, they kept quiet and returned to their homes. Next morning, when the forester, on his way to the forest, was passing through the village, the villagers stopped him, saying he had not obtained any permission to pass through the village. It was now the forester, who got stunned. He immediately understood how impractical he was yesterday and sportingly took the befitting retaliation by the tribal villagers. He told them smilingly that they could pass through the forest to go to the pump house. The tribal villagers had their own way to handle such situations.

CHAPTER - 6

Human Resource Development And Building Institutions

It is now well established through research that no country with an educated, technically trained, labour force is poor, and no country with a predominantly illiterate, untrained labour force is rich. It has also been seen that investment in education and training produces very high internal rates of return. Especially high are the returns to basic literacy. The rate of returns to investment in schooling is in the neighbour hood of 50 per cent per year in many rich countries, and in developing countries like India, the rate of return to primary schooling is even higher. Any poor country or a region within a country that wants to develop could do no better than use its scarce resources in schools, technical education, training and management (Singh, 1999: 99-101).

At Sadguru, we realised fairly soon after we launched our activities that unless we empower and develop the local people and build their own institutions and organizations, no development effort or initiative can be successful and sustainable. Accordingly, we accorded a high priority to human resource development and institution building. In this chapter, I describe the activities of Sadguru in these two areas and their impact on the quality of life of local people.

Empowerment of People

The tribal people in the Sadguru's project area are mainly Bhils, which is one of the Scheduled Tribes (ST) in India. Bhils tribe represents third largest schedule tribes in our country, mainly concentrated in the central-west India tribal belt. In the past, the tribal people in this area were dependent on the forest for their livelihood and so was the case in other tribal regions. As forests have largely disappeared from this area and the forest land is owned by the State, local people slowly took to subsistence farming in order to eke out their livelihood. In general, the level of literacy in the project area is lower and the incidence of poverty higher as compared to the non-tribal areas. Due to poverty the nutrition level of people is very low. They are at the bottom of human development index. Women have to bear the brunt of collecting fuel-wood and fodder and fetching drinking water and also of doing various inter-cultural operations in crops. There are no non-farm employment opportunities available in the area. Excessive population growth has aggravated the scarcity of food, fuel wood, and fodder in the area. Consequently, people have to migrate seasonally to urban areas in the State as well as in other States in search of wage-paid jobs so as to support their families. Thus, the quality of the rural labour force in the Sadguru's project area was poor in terms of skills, education, training, values and attitudes. There is a positive correlation between literacy rate and real per capita gross domestic product. The poor quality of rural labour force in conjunction with very low per capita availability of capital explains to a large extent the low productivity and hence low per capita incomes in the project area. Sadguru conceptualized and developed its human resource development activities keeping in view these characteristics of the local people.

The philosophy of Sadguru is to empower people with a view to enable them to initiate and implement development programmes on their own and eventually make the programmes sustainable. With this objective, Sadguru has taken up several measures including awareness creation and training of villagers- both men and women. With the implementation of lift irrigation (LI) schemes, the nature of participation changes as the emphasis shifts from technical aspects to organizational and managerial aspects with much more time and effort devoted to training leaders, secretaries, and operators to manage the scheme in a technically and economically viable and self-sustaining manner. The Sadguru team under the aegis of its Cooperative Cell starts imparting training to member families in various aspects like operation and management of the scheme, water pricing, water distribution, keeping records and accounts and so on.

We started our work based on the premise that for success of any rural development programme, it is necessary that the people involved are empowered with technical and legal information, education and training so that they can meaningfully participate in the programme and are able to take it over from the sponsoring organization in due course of time. Sadguru has done this job very successfully by conscientising and organizing farmers into formal and non-formal organizations and handing over its schemes to the people's organizations. Sadguru has also been promoting entrepreneurship among the tribals through implementation of its various other activities. Besides, as a result of Sadguru's activities, lots of opportunities have been created for development of local leadership which in turn has enhanced their involvement in making decisions relating to various governments' sponsored rural development programmes that affect their well being. Training and extension activities have empowered the village communities who now are more knowledgeable, self-reliant and confident.

Village level government functionaries and farmers are involved in agricultural extension through creating awareness, imparting training in various skills and sharing knowledge. Special efforts are made for ensuring women participation in agricultural extension services as they do 50-60 per cent of the farm work. Training in land and water management and other development activities is imparted to the people and functionaries of local institutions. Follow up of training is also carried out to make sure that new and existing village functionaries do their jobs efficiently.

It was realized from past experiences that the training and motivation is an important component of rural development projects at the grassroots level. Therefore, training forms the basis of the Sadguru model. Later, the need was felt to start a training and research institute for further strengthening the model by way of meeting Sadguru's own training needs and imparting training to other NG0s and government agencies working in similar fields. Promotion of women's groups by ensuring their active involvement in the development process receives a high priority in the programme activities. Thus, for example, Ll Cooperatives (LICS) and other programmes have helped members to articulate their needs and to emerge as a more effective demand system than the existing institutions such as the Large Area Multi-Purpose Co-operative Societies (LAMPS).

Sadguru has done a pioneering work in its project area in empowering women through training. I now briefly describe Sadguru's activities in that field and their impact.

Women's Empowerment and Participation

Tribal women play an important role in on-farm and off-farm activities in the area. Except ploughing the fields, they are involved in almost all the farm activities. No development is possible in the area without their empowerment and participation. Realizing this, Sadguru attaches a high priority to women's empowerment and development through training. Women are trained as manad sevikas (honorary), masons, construction supervisors on lift irrigation and check dams, birth attendants, trainers, organizers, farm managers, and off-farm income earners.

In every LIC, out of eleven members of the Executive Body, at least three are women. Thus, they are involved in LIC's decision making processes and management.

In the watershed development programmes also, women are directly involved in decision making processes including selection of activities to be carried out on their agricultural lands. Women from the community are also selected as village level volunteers by the community themselves to implement this programme.

The farm forestry and agro forestry programmes are entirely implemented by women. All the activities such as nursery raising, pits digging and plantation are exclusively carried out by women who are trained and guided from time to time. Many of the field supervisors in the forestry programme are women, mainly drawn from the local community. Women also play an important role in the village level JFM committees and participate in decision making and protection of forests. In JFM 50 % of managing committee members are women.

Under the biogas programme, women are trained as masons to construct biogas plants in villages. After training, they do the job very well and most of them are earning Rs. 5000-6000/- every year as biogas masons by constructing 10-12 biogas plants. This shows that tribal women have both entrepreneurship and technical capability in this field. They also do the necessary follow up to ensure proper working of the biogas plants.

It is only the women who take up the off-farm income generating activities of Sadguru in the project area. Though limited to a few villages at present, the programme has been successful in supplementing farm incomes and making productive use of the women's leisure time. Some of the women participate in exhibitions organised at state and national levels every year and earn good incomes from the sale of their products.

Many women have been trained as Traditional Birth Attendants (TBA) and Manad Sevikas (honorary health workers or animators) under the preventive health care programme. This activity was started in 1985, but now the emphasis has been shifted to training programmes conducted centrally in a newly established training institute and this programme has been declining.

Sadguru has implemented one of the four pilot projects initiated by the INDISCO - International Labour Organization (INDISCO - ILO) in four selected states of India in 1994. Under this project, informal women's groups were formed in INDISCO (funded by ILO) project villages. Special emphasis was given to women involvement in village activities. Twenty such women's groups had been formed by the end of June 1997 under this scheme. These women's groups have been assisting villagers in taking up income generating activities and also mobilizing funds for savings and credit schemes. Two dairy co-operatives supported by the District Co-operative Milk Producers' Union had been started by one women's group in a village where a lift irrigation co-operative already existed. The ILO Project came to an end in 1999, after five years, but, the activity still continues by women groups.

As a result of human resource development initiatives, most

of the activities of Sadguru now are managed by formal and informal people's institutions which were all established and nurtured by Sadguru in the process of implementing its activities. Building up a strong and sustainable institutional framework was instrumental in the widespread adoption of Sadguru's appropriate technologies. Sadguru's success story is a result of devotion to its resources and attention to human empowerment of local people, and building up a strong institutional foundation.

From the year 1996 to 2003, Sadguru has provided training and capacity inputs to as many as 41,268 participants which also includes exposure and learning visit to Sadguru. The total numbers of training programmes organised during the above period was 1,591.

The intensive and magnitude of training programmes have resulted in equipping and empowering the village people and community in undertaking and managing various programmes on sustainable basis.

As a result of Sadguru's empowerment activities, men and women in its project area have developed confidence in their ability and skills to undertake various income generating activities.

Building People's Institutions and Organizations

Agricultural and rural development is influenced by a multitude of factors such as natural resources, human resources (labour), capital, technology, and institutions and organizations. The terms `organization' and `institution' are often used interchangeably. We consider organizations as a subset of the broader set of institutional structures or arrangements. An organization connotes coordinated act or endeavour of two or more individuals. It is created to give effect to a certain institutional arrangement.

Institutions and organizations are important aids to development. They may influence agricultural and rural development in many different ways including provision of production inputs and services, reduction of transaction costs, enhancement of bargaining power of rural producers vis-a-vis those to whom they sell their produce and from whom they buy production inputs and services, influencing investments and savings and bringing the two together, and so on. The economic life of any community takes place in a milieu of organizations and institutions. They largely determine the economic structure of the community and set the rules in which the economic game is played. Changes in these organizations and institutions over time will probably have a pronounced effect on economic output and developments. Often these effects are difficult to isolate and measure because of the interdependence between changes in organizations and institutions, and between other instrument variables of agricultural development (Singh, 1999: 107-108).

Building people's institutions and enhancing their capacity are the main strengths of the Sadguru model. Sadguru has created a large number of people's institutions for undertaking different types of activities which the villagers find appropriate. The institutions are both formal and non-formal depending on the nature of the activities involved and people's preferences. The formal institutions are registered irrigation co-operatives, registered milk producers' co-operatives, registered forest co-operatives and women horticulture cooperatives. The non-formal institutions consist of Mahila Mandalsl Juths, Self Help Groups (SHGs. and youth groups. At the end of March 2004, there were 1,041 formal institutions and non-formal ones in the project area (Table 6.2).

Table 6.2 : Types and Number of Formal and Non-formal Institutions set up by Sadguru in its Project Area as of December 2004

Nature of Village Institutions	Total Number of VIs existing Members	Total
Lift Irrigation Cooperatives	243	19,156
Watershed Associations	41	16,154
Informal self help groups under	558	7,955

watershed, agriculture extension, forestry, L.I., CD, Swa shakti, SAHAJ and other activities.		
Youth and Farmers groups – CD, L.I., Watershed and other activities	118	1,687
Women horticulture groups	267	12,222
Joint forest management cooperatives	27	4,339
Total	**1254**	**61,513**

Usually, to begin with an informal village group is formed to initiate an activity in a selected village and to mobilise the people. The next step is to assess and make an inventory of the village resources and determine the willingness of people to participate in the activity. In many cases, local leaders, elderly people, village panchayat representatives and village level government functionaries are of great help in assessing the resources available and initiating various programme activities. Informal groups are formed to start watershed and afforestation activities. The groups help the Sadguru team chalk out appropriate strategies to develop, use and manage the available resources efficiently for the benefit of the village people.

Community management, particularly, post project management by the community is imperative for the successful and sustainable management of the activities and the assets created. In its basic philosophy and approach from the very beginning, it was clear to Sadguru Foundation and made clear to the community that the post project management of each and every programme would be by the community itself under some formal or informal institutional arrangements as may be decided by the community itself. Consistent with this policy, all the programmes have been managed by the community in case of common programmes and by the respective households in case of household oriented programmes. Various types of village institutions, formal and informal have come up to implement and manage the programmes.

Now I briefly describe the roles, functions and impacts of various types of institutions set up by Sadguru in its project area.

Lift Irrigation Cooperatives

Lift Irrigation Cooperatives (LICs) are the most important of all the people's institutions created and nurtured by Sadguru in its Project area. As of December 2004, 243 Lift Irrigation Cooperatives had been established in the area. They differ in their age, size and impact. There are also significant variations in their operating rules and norms, the rates charged for water, and the managerial practices followed. LICs depend on Sadguru for guidance and support in the initial stages, but they become increasingly autonomous as they mature, taking their decisions and sorting out their problems themselves. In most of the LICS, operational responsibility is entrusted to the paid secretary who reports to the elected management committee of the LIC. Many LICs also employ paid water distributors and watchmen. LICs now keep their account books on their own. This gives an opportunity to the interested members of the LICs to go through these books and ask questions if they so desire. This is a healthy tradition adopted by the people themselves to detect irregularities, if any, in the system. This fosters the norms of autonomy, transparency, and accountability among the LICS. However, in co-operatives where their secretaries are not well versed with the writing and keeping of accounts, Sadguru staff help them in these matters, in initial stage. (This happens in a village where even VIII passed Secretary is not available.)

Even when LICs become mature and self-sustaining, they continue to face problems, challenges and new opportunities. To deal with all of their problems including repair and maintenance, the first federation was set up for Jhalod taluka for 56 primary irrigation cooperatives as of 31.03.2004. Such federations in other talukas are in the process of formulation. Sadguru is trying to strengthen the federation by persuading those LICs which are not yet affiliated to it to become its members and to utilize its services. Sadguru has also deputed some of its technical staff to work with the federation who are paid by the Federation. Previously, LICs were dependent on the guidance and support of Sadguru. But now the LICs are capable of sorting out their problems with the help of hired technicians. Even where formal federation is not formed, informal federation consisting of primary L. I. Cooperatives has been in operation providing effective services to the member cooperatives. Sadguru keeps in touch with most of the LICs in one way or other through such formal and informal federations. In order to enhance the spirit of fraternity among all cooperatives atleast once a year a general gathering of all L.I. Cooperatives in each taluka takes place and their federation also meet once in a year in the premises of Sadguru.

As desired by the communities themselves, all the community lift irrigation schemes are managed by duly registered cooperatives. All the cooperatives are functioning in accordance with the statutory provisions. These cooperatives have been managing the irrigation systems fairly well and fulfilling all of their obligations. By and large, these irrigation cooperatives have displayed great sense of responsibility. The best part is that without any subsidy towards the operational cost, these cooperatives have managed their affairs by charging full costs to the member farmers. There may be occasional delays in the payment of water charges by the farmers, but, everyone has to pay before the next irrigation season, otherwise defaulting farmers would not get the irrigation.

Often these cooperatives have levied penalty on the defaulters. An example of Mota Dharola cooperative is something that needs to be shared in this context. In the first season of its commissioning, many farmers did not pay their dues in time and there was a lot of delay in making the payments. The farmers had earned handsomely on account of irrigation, and therefore, the managing committee of the cooperative got annoyed with the defaulting farmers. It was a powerful and gutsy committee. They levied a penalty of Rs. 100/- per day for the delayed payment. If the farmers original amount was Rs. 500/- and if he delayed the payment by five days, he would be required to pay Rs. 500/- more over and above his original due. This rather drastic penalty proved to be a great deterrent and from the next season there were no defaults in the payment of water dues. I have never heard of such a drastic penalty having been imposed by a managing committee, and more interestingly the decision duly accepted by the farmers. Our ruling elite and the managers of the government irrigation systems should note this.

Box 6.1 depicts a story of a successful lift irrigation cooperative society and impact on the village economy and Box 6.2 illustrate how a poor tribal helps the rich farmers in his village by supplying irrigation water from his well.

Box 6.1 - Irrigation Day Becoming An Annual Festival Day in Degawada Village

In village Degawada of Limkheda Taluka, Dahod District, a community lift irrigation system was constructed in the year 1994 - 1995 and was successfully commissioned on 7th January 1995 in the presence of entire village community. Since then, a Lift Irrigation Cooperative Society, constituted by the farmers concerned, has been managing the irrigation system very satisfactorily. Availability of irrigation has substantially improved the economic condition of the community. The community, which was once poor and without any food security, today has become self-sufficient in fulfilling its basic needs. There have also been other developments in their lives including a sharp increase in the literacy rate. The community attributes their progress to the irrigation system. So much so that the entire village community, every year celebrates 7th January as an annual festival. On that day, the cooperative members decorate the Pump House, hoist the National Flag and sing Bhajans (hymns) throughout the night. Their prayers also include thanking Sadguru for bringing prosperity and peace in their lives. What irrigation means to poor communities is reflected through this experience. The community has managed their system so well and efficiently that they have created a reserve fund of Rs. 1,50,000/- from their profit, which is a very big amount considering that the system is small and operates on the principle of no-profit-no-loss.

Horticulture Women Groups

The horticulture activities have been organised and taken up by formal and informal women groups, which are federated at the block level. These groups have their managing committees and general bodies, which take necessary decisions for implementation and post-project management of the programme. There were about 267 such village institutions / groups having 12,222 members involved in this activity at the end of December 2004. These groups are involved in planning of activities, nursery raising, plantation, protection, etc.

Box 6.2 - Generosity of a tribal farmer

> *Somabhai is a farmer of Chitrodia village. He raised a forest nursery near his well under Sadguru's nursery raising programme and earned Rs. 22,000/-. He was happy with his earning and decided to do something for the community. Whereas he earned a handsome amount from the nursery, other farmers in the village were suffering from the adverse effects of a drought, particularly, due to the acute fodder shortage. He decided to give water from his well to the nearby farmers and provided irrigation to ten acres of the land of twenty farmers almost free of cost by charging only the actual diesel cost. From the water provided, the farmers got green fodder worth about Rs. 60,000/-, which helped them sustain their animals during the drought year. In addition, he allowed the villagers to take water from his well for drinking purpose and also constructed a trough for the purpose of providing drinking water for the village animals, another great gesture by the tribal farmer. In progressive areas like Rajkot and other places, when rich farmers are making huge profit by selling water, here is a tribal farmer showing concern towards the community and sharing his wealth with others without any profit consideration.*

Watershed Associations

Micro watershed projects of Sadguru are all managed by the Watershed Associations and Watershed Committees formed by such associations under the guidelines of the Government of India. The entire programme of watershed development is managed by these watershed committees, who are accountable and responsible to the Watershed Associations. The watershed development programme has several users groups and self help groups, which are all performing well.

Women Self Help Groups (SHGs)

As of December 2004, there were more than 558 SHGs of women in our project villages. Many of them are in watershed development projects. These women self-help groups have demonstrated good strength in their operation and many of them have developed linkages with the financial institutions and adopted various income generating activities and other entrepreneurial endeavours. Many such women groups have established good linkages with the lift irrigation, horticulture and vegetable cultivation programmes in their respective villages. In 2003, in the State Level evaluation of World Bank supported Swa-Shakti women programme, these self-help groups were evaluated as among the best by virtue of their performance. Similarly in 2003, a study of these women self-help groups was conducted by IRMA faculty, which very much admired the functioning and performance of these women SHG groups. BASIX, a premiere micro finance institute in India, also carried out a study of these groups and appreciated their functioning.

Joint Forest Management Groups

The joint forest management programme is managed jointly by the community, forest department and the NGO. The community plays the major role in the development of forests and its protection under the aegis of the Forest Protection Committees (FPCs) concerned. As of March 2004, 27 Joint Forest Management Groups / FPCs had been organized and most of them were working successfully.

Federations

Some of our major village institutions have been federated at the block and taluka levels. Two such village institutions are lift irrigation cooperatives and horticulture groups. Prominent among them by virtue of their being a formal federation is the Lift Irrigation Federation of Jhalod. This federation consists of about 56 member lift irrigation cooperatives. All the member cooperatives of the Federation are very happy with its functioning. Perhaps, it may be the only federation of its kind in any of the tribal regions of our country. Apart from fulfilling its obligations towards the member cooperatives, this federation has diversified into various other related activities, a rare development attained by any such federation of the tribal cooperatives. The federation has got the dealership of Jain Irrigation System for distribution and installation of drip and sprinkler irrigation systems. Not only the federation obtained this dealership, it has now become an expert in the installation of these systems. The premiere company, Jain Irrigation, has given a certificate that the workers of federation are the best in the installation of drip irrigation system. They are all young tribal boys duly trained by the federation. Another important diversification of this federation is in the development of common wasteland successfully. Yet, another important contribution and diversification of this irrigation federation is in the area of drinking water. In three of its member villages, it has installed drinking water facilities, collaborating with the primary irrigation cooperatives concerned. These drinking water facilities are managed by women groups and they pay fully for this facility. More such drinking water supply schemes are planned and being executed by the federation.

In conclusion, it must be mentioned that, by and large, these village institutions have proved very strong and as a result their activities have been sustained over a considerably long period of time. For example, our oldest lift irrigation cooperative has been operating successfully for more than 28 years. So is case with a large numbers of other cooperatives, operating successfully for 15-27 years. No where in our country can one find more than 200 community lift irrigation cooperatives successfully managed by the tribals themselves.

Training and Capacity Building

There are very few NGOs who give priority and weightage to the training as given by Sadguru. The progress and performance of Sadguru could be attributed to such high and constant priority to the training. No organization can afford to ignore the training of its workers and the users groups. However, one must remember that training is neither a panacea for all ills, nor it is a waste of time. Its true value is somewhere in between these two extreme views. What is important is to know what training can or cannot do and acquire skills in designing and conducting training effectively and economically for the capacity building and improved performance.

The Sadguru Training Institute

After having accumulated nearly 20 years of valuable and intensive experience in the field of rural and tribal development with particular focus on natural resources development and management, Sadguru thought it appropriate to widely share and disseminate its experience and expertise through an institutionalized system of training and documentation. With this purpose in mind, it was envisaged to set up a training and research institute. This vision was actualized with the establishment of a Training and Research Institute at village Chosala near Dahod in 1995.

The Institute is intended to fulfill the following main objectives:

- To enhance the capacity of Saduru's partners and other NGOs in the area of natural resource management (NRM) and other related areas through formal theoretical and field trainings and exposure visits;

- To provide training and consultancy services to NGOs and other organizations engaged in NRM;

- To promote and expand government involvement in NRM projects;

- To document successful experiences of Sadguru in the field of rural and tribal development and to undertake problem-solving action-oriented studies as and when necessary; and

- To help improve the design and implementation of public policies and programmes in NRM through advocacy and lobbying.

The Institute has excellent physical infrastructure and facilities. It has well equipped residential facilities, classrooms, conference halls, syndicate rooms, a boardroom, an auditorium, a library and reading room, a common room for recreation and a hall for indoor games, along with demonstrative field activities such as L. I. Schemes, check dams, horticulture, drip irrigation, floriculture, etc., in the training institute premises itself, providing instant exposure to the visitors visiting even for couple of hours.

That Sadguru attaches great importance to training as a means of human resource development is evident from the fact it expended Rs. 3.18 million on training and supporting activities in 2002-2003. This constituted nearly 4 % of the total programme expenditure in the year under reference. It has created a reasonably good infrastructure for training including a modern training institute equipped with state-of the -art equipment and facilities. The trainers comprise highly qualified and experienced staff drawn from both within and outside the organization. Its expertise in conducting field-oriented training programmes in areas such as water harvesting through small check dams, organizing and managing cooperative lift irrigation schemes, participatory micro watershed management, organizing self-help groups of women, agro-forestry, agriculture and horticulture has been widely recognized all over India by both GOs and NGOs. Participants in various training courses organised by it have rated the courses offered to be of high quality. This has been possible due mainly to the high emphasis that is placed by the organization on the quality and affordability of the programmes. Many of Sadguru staff are well qualified to be trainers or faculty at the post graduate level in the respective discipline.

Several foreign students and interns have undergone training at Sadguru. It has conducted training programmes in small water harvesting structures and organised exposure visits in agro-forestry and horticulture for groups of Ethiopians under a Triangular Cooperation Project between India, Ethiopia and Norway. Within India, several Sate governments sponsor their officers including IAS officers for exposure visits to Sadguru. An idea of the number of training programmes conducted by Sadguru over the period,

1996-2003, and the number of participants who attended the programmes could be had through a glance at Figure 6.1.

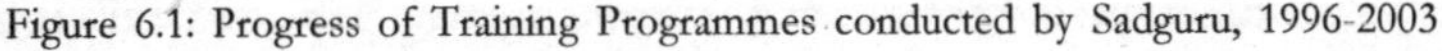
Figure 6.1: Progress of Training Programmes conducted by Sadguru, 1996-2003

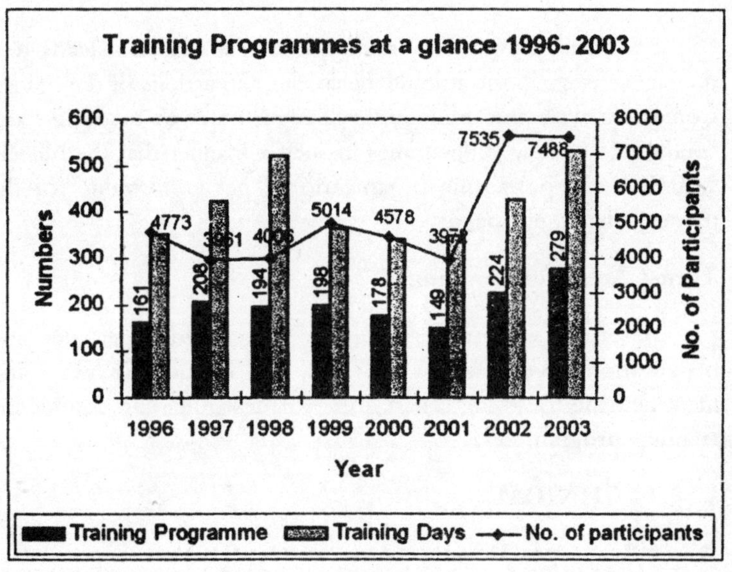

The following are some of the special features, which make the Sadguru Training Institute a centre of excellence in the field of training in NRM for the grassroots level:

- Excellent physical infrastructure and facilities;
- Well equipped lecture halls, syndicate rooms, and an auditrium;
- Pollution-free serene rural environment conducive to learning and reflection;
- Easy access to field-based innovative projects;
- An optimum mix of theory and practice;
- Well-trained and experienced faculty;
- High credibility of Sadguru buttressed by its 30 years of

experience in rural / tribal development through natural resource management;

➢ A functional mechanism for exchange of' 'lab- to-field' and' field-to-lab' knowledge, ideas, and experiences.

Sadguru believes that training is useful only if it leads to a desirable change in the attitude, behaviour and actions of the trainee. Consistent with this philosophy, Sadguru strives to design and conduct its training programmes in such a manner that the trainees as well their sponsoring organizations "get good value for the money" that they spend.

Thrust Areas for Training

Based on Sadguru's rich and diverse field experience and observations over the last 30 years, the Training Institute has identified the following thrust areas for designing and conducting training programmes:

I. TECHNICAL

Water Resources Development

- Planning, design and execution of community lift irrigation projects;
- Planning, design and execution of water harvesting struck tures;
- Development of surface water resources; and
- Ground water recharge and resource utilization.

Micro Watershed Development

- Participatory planning, design and execution of soil and moisture conservation projects;
- Resource inventory; and
- Application of remote sensing in natural resource manage ment.

Forestry

- Promotion of agro and farm forestry;
- Design and execution of community forestry interventions; and
- Joint Forest management

Agricultural and Horticultural Development and Extension

- Promotion of adoption of latest practices in agricultural and horticultural development and management;
- Orchard development in semi-arid areas;
- Promotion of floriculture; and
- Promotion of adoption of scientific methods of water use and management.

II. ECONOMIC

- Promotion of off-farm Income Generating enterprises;
- Mobilising and utilizing small savings through self-help groups of women; and
- Marketing of Farm and Non-farm products.

III. SOCIAL/ INSTITUTIONAL

- Community watershed management
- Institutionalization of water users groups
- Participatory forest management
- Micro credit and savings groups
- Participatory irrigation management

IV. ORGANIZATION AND MANAGEMENT

- Development of indicators of monitoring and evaluation of NRM programmes;

- Management of lift irrigation cooperatives; and
- Management of NGOs.

V. Gender in NRM

- Gender sensitisation; and
- Mainstreaming gender in NRM

Training programmes offered in these areas are of the following three types:

- General programmes open to any interested prospective participant;
- Tailor-made programmes designed in response to demands from prospective sponsors; and
- In-house training programmes designed for the staff of Sadguru and its partner organisations.

The Training Institute has played an important role in equipping the members of Management Committees of village institutions with the knowledge and skills required for fulfilling their obligations.

From the very beginning, the training courses offered by the Institute aimed at capacity building of the community and the village institutions and their functionaries. Continued efforts have been made for the capacity building of the community and various village institutions. The satisfactory management and sustainability of various programmes and village institutions are the result of such continued efforts in capacity building.

With the expansion of Sadguru's activities, the need to provide training to various groups also increased for both post-project management of the projects and for project implementation. With this arouse the need to share and disseminate our knowledge and experiences with other groups to enable them to replicate the programme. The setting up of training institute has helped in strengthening the training programmes and capacity building of various groups within the project area and outside. The personnel working in governmental and non-governmental organizations from 17 Indian States take benefit of Sadguru's training programmes on regular basis. The most important aspect of this training institute and its training programmes is the field -oriented training programmes. As the training institute is run by the practicing NGO and the area of activities of NGO is around the training institute, groups coming for training and exposure get the first hand knowledge of the successful activities of Sadguru in various fields including NRM. As and when necessary, external resource persons are also invited to supplement the training and capacity building efforts. It has continuous institutional linkages with premiere institutes like IRMA which helps in bringing in qualitative improvement in the training programmes as well as upgrading Sadguru's training institute.

Examples of village institutions functioning well for several years and their federations becoming not only successful, but diversifying their activities successfully are rare indeed in India. This is the type of rural development seldom seen in any other tribal regions in India and is a testimony of the successful efforts and inputs provided by Sadguru for capacity building of the communities and their institutions.

More than 18,930 people attending Sadguru's various training programmes and coming to Sadguru on the exposure visits in last three years speak a lot about the growing popularity of Sadguru's training programmes and that of Sadguru's various successful activities in NRM.

A Sample of Participants' Feedback

A few of the feedbacks received from the participants in Sadguru's training programmes are reproduced below:

"Very happy to see the way Sadguru and its campus have come up. Visit to Sadguru is a development pilgrimage to me".

"A very happy and friendly environment, very conducive to training and learning. The hospitality and attention given by the staff was very touching".

"The knowledge and confidence of trainers is very high. The combination of theory and practical aspects used in the training programmes is excellent, something which has not been seen anywhere else".

"This has been an eye opening visit for us. Our work is related to WATER so this learning helped us in broadening our understanding of various aspects of water and related issues.. This is one place where we need to come back".

"Sadguru is like a HEAVEN on this earth."

Networking and Public Advocacy

Sadguru has deliberately followed a policy of supporting other small and new NGOs engaged in NRM. Several NG0s in the project area are now assisted by Sadguru in building their capacity. This is a new development consistent with Sadguru's present strategy to encourage small NGOs to collaborate with it in its various activities. The results of the support to small and new NGOs are mixed, but, encouraging so far. Some have grown well and few others have not progressed well. Largely the leadership of such NGOs has made a difference. However, on the whole, this approach has proved very helpful and such collaboration with other NGOs has in turn helped strengthening the Sadguru model and extended its scope and coverage. It is envisaged that with Sadguru's guidance and technical support, small NGOs will grow in strength over time and will prove to be effective instruments for the development and management of land and water resources in their areas. This approach is consistent with the Sadguru's strategic planning and many funding organisations also endorse this approach.

In India, non-government organizations (NGOs) have undertaken considerable work in the field of natural resource management (NRM). Their work has focused primarily on grassroots action, often ignoring the larger environment. The poor and the disadvantaged sections of the society, who are most affected by the NRM policies and legislation are voiceless with limited bargaining power to influence the state. In the past, NGOs have tried to raise their voices against the vast gap that exists between publicly stated intentions as expressed in government policies and legislation, and the actual practice on behalf of the impoverished and marginalized communities. But, they had limited success in influencing the state policies and legislation related to NRM. In the context of globalization, however, there has been a gradual change in the nature of relationship between the state and NGOs. With growing realization among NGOs about the role of macro level forces in shaping the grassroots action, NGOs have emerged as important actors who influence the process of formulation and implementation of the public policy in the NRM sector.

On the other hand, with growing interest on the part of the government to work with the NGO, opportunities for influencing public policies in the NRM sector have also increased. Hence with this realization and opportunities, advocacy has emerged as an important area for the NGOs' work in the recent years. Capacity building of NGOs for undertaking public advocacy is very important. However, only a few organizations, such as ACTIONAID, Institute of Rural Management, Anand (IRMA), National Advocacy Studies Institute, Pune, and a few others have conducted some workshops and training programmes on public advocacy for the NGOs. Sadguru's training institute has planned for constant public advocacy efforts in NRM through occasional workshops and networking of like-minded organizations. Such workshop, a rare development of its own kind offering in-detail inputs of advocacy, specifically for NGOs working in the NRM sector are expected to be useful in the present day context.

Over the 30 years, Sadguru has successfully used Public Advocacy as an instrument of persuading the Government of Gujarat and Government of India to effect the pro-poor changes in their policies, particularly in the field of water resource development and management. For example: (i) Sadguru persuaded the Gujarat Electricity Board (GEB) to change its power tariff from flat rates to unit based metered tariff ; (ii) change in the proportion of contribution required from project beneficiaries ; (iii) change in watershed development guidelines ; and (iv) permission for water lifting from the Government reservoirs and canals situated in the tribal regions in Gujarat. For sometime Sadguru had been thinking of setting up an informal forum for policy advocacy, known as Environment Conservation Forum (ECF). The Forum was eventually launched on April 1999. Since then it has been actively working in the region to facilitate NRM efforts of the NGOs, Forest Department and Village Institutions.

While working with its partners, ECF has realized the importance of enabling the partners to understand basic concepts and strategies of public advocacy so that they could play an active role in influencing public policies in the NRM sector. Hence, Sadguru conducts workshops on Building Capacity for Public Advocacy in Natural Resource Management in collaboration with IRMA. Those stakeholders in NRM who are interested to take up advocacy, such as government officers, NGOs and funding agencies participate in these workshops.

CHAPTER - 7

Managing Relationship With Various Partners

Rural development is multi-disciplinary and multi-agency. To be successful, a rural development project requires cooperation and collaboration of several organizations and inputs from several disciplines. I realized this immediately after my entry into the area of rural development. After training as a social scientist and heading the Human Resources Development Department in a company, I had no problems in establishing fruitful relations with various governmental organizations (GOs) and departments at the district and the state levels and maintaining good working relationship with them. In fact, this is now considered a major strength of Sadguru, which most NGOs in India lack. There are umpteen examples of how Sadguru was able to mobilize financial support from GOs and national and international donors based on its credibility and good relationship with GOs and NGOs. In this chapter, I will share some of these experiences.

Governmental Organizations

Government has been and continues to be an important organization in the field of agricultural and rural development in India. Development is seen as the responsibility of the government in all developing countries. But when one talks of dealing with government organizations the usual reactions include feelings of frustration, and acrimony and stories of indifference and delays on the part of GOs. The relationships between the two are characterized by mutual distrust and antagonism towards each other. I have always believed that both GOs and NGOs have an important role to play in rural development, therefore, it is imperative that these two important agencies co-exist, support and cooperate with each other. Indian NGOs, or the voluntary sector in India, has a very long history of involvement in socio-economic development of people. In fact social reformers and philanthropists have rendered their services, particularly to its poor and disadvantaged section. Eminent people like Mahatma Gandhi, Sardar Patel, Thakkar Bapa and Jai Prakash Narayan served the people of India selflessly. This image and respect for voluntary work and voluntary workers has, however, has recently suffered a downside. Government agencies and the voluntary sector view each other with skepticism.

Sadguru, however, has a different story to tell about its relationship and partnerships with the Government. We have progressed and benefited because of our long-standing partnerships with the Government. We began our work with Government support and continue to receive it. However, we have relied more on the bureaucrats for the support rather than the politicians. Bureaucrats have had no difficulty in supporting us because of our apolitical status. I do have to say, on some occasions, on some serious matters of policy issue, we did successfully garner support from MLAs and MPs, the ministers and even chief ministers. But, normally, we chose to work through bureaucrats. To state an example, it was K. G. Ramnathan, Special Secretary, Rural development, Government of Gujarat, who was instrumental in granting us an approval for the first three lift irrigation schemes despite the stiff resistance put up by the Superintending Engineer of Irrigation Department. He not only encouraged Sadguru to enter into the field of irrigation, but also opened up the avenue for the NGO sector. The support continued at the district level as well. Once our credibility was established support from the bureaucrats came easily. In Gujarat, at the district level, a large number of schemes were approved and on regular basis huge amounts were made available because of the institutionalization of our relationship in a good environment.

For the last several years, we have been working in Madhya Pradesh and Rajasthan. In Madhya Pradesh we got involved in rural development in 1989 after great efforts. A senior bureaucrat, V. G. Nigam, invited us to work in Jhabua district of the State. It was very difficult to enter into Madhya Pradesh in the field of lift irrigation because the Irrigation Department, particularly, the Madhya Pradesh Lift Irrigation Corporation had given a bad account of itself in the field. Therefore, every time we put up a proposal for a lift irrigation scheme in Jhabua, the Irrigation Department turned it down saying that the lift irrigation schemes were not feasible and viable. Eventually, two officers, P. Joy Oommen and P. D. Meena, helped us in cutting the ice in Madhya Pradesh, and cleared our proposals for lift irrigation schemes for Jhabua under the Madhya Pradesh Antyavasayee Sahkari Vikas Nigam Ltd. We again faced some hurdles created by the technical department in granting the sanction for the first two schemes. Those two schemes were to be constructed on tanks. The Executive Engineer told us that there was no question of technical sanction to these schemes as both the tanks were not existing in the area. We said, we had surveyed the area and we had seen the tanks. As the existing records and their topo-sheets and other documents, did not locate them therefore, he was right and we were wrong. We requested him to accompany us to see them but, he was extremely reluctant for that as well. We had to ultimately request him to give us in writing that these tanks were non-existent. Suddenly he told us to come back after couple of hours so that he could have some more time to locate those tanks in his records. When we met him after two hours, he conceded the existence of these two tanks.

We faced some difficulty in working in Madhya Pradesh. Till now we have installed only 15 community lift irrigation schemes in Jhabua. We were expecting to expand the programme in Jhabua, but, have not been able to gather support. We have found it difficult to institutionalize the relationship with Madhya Pradesh government.

Our experiences in Rajasthan have been fairly good and encouraging. By and large, Rajasthan has responded well by supporting us. We have come across several bureaucrats in Rajasthan, who have been to extremely supportive. Our area of operation in Rajasthan earlier was Banswara district and now we have been able to extend it to Jhalawar district, with modest beginning in Chittorgarh district (Pratapgarh sub-division). To give an example of our goodwill which helped us spread our wings in

Rajasthan. Convinced of our work the then Collector of Banswara spoke to the Commissioner, Salaluddin Ahmed, recommended us to him. In September 1995, Salaluddin Ahméd telephoned and enquired that why we were not doing much work in Banswara. I said we wanted financial support from the Government. He asked me to submit a proposal for the support. I fixed him a summary of the proposal costing around Rs. 5.25 crore for 45 small-scale water resources projects immediately. Our proposal was approved by fax immediately in principle and I was asked to visit his office within a week with the detailed proposal and to sign an agreement.

Relationship and experiences of Sadguru with the Government.

I would like to quote the following phrases from a study conducted in September 2000 by Prof. Anil Bhatt, formerly Professor, Indian Institute of Management, Ahmedabad.

"Sadguru's relationship with Government in general, but with Tribal Development and Rural Development departments in particular has been so strong that sometimes officers have asked Sadguru to start the work in anticipation of approvals and sanctions and Sadguru has readily done so".

"Unlike most other GO-NGO relationships, Sadguru's relationship with government is much beyond the donor-donee relationship. Sadguru has not only carried out projects for the government but effectively influenced government policies and procedures".

"There is a mutuality in the relationship. Sadguru is participating in government's advisory and decision making bodies, carries out studies, evaluations and trainings and prepares proposal for the government for international funding as well as participates in government delegations abroad"..

"Sadguru has continuously and in many instances successfully influenced government programmes, policies, procedures and practices".

"Sadguru has continuously influenced the government both from outside

and from within as a member of several government bodies. It has tried to influence specific government policies, procedures and practices as also government's thinking about NGOs and its relationship with NGOs in general".

"In 1995, Sadguru along with other prominent NGOs was instrumental in persuading the government to simplify and liberalize the procedures for approval of water resources schemes. Government also agreed that technical as well as administrative approvals for scheme up to Rs. two million will be given by the district level officers which was till then done at the state level".

"Another reason for such good partnership, the officials felt was the excellent performance of Sadguru. Sadguru's work was unanimously acknowledged to be of very high quality. A very senior government official that we talked to honestly admitted that Sadguru's work was far superior to that of the government. A Secretary in the Water Resources Development Department said that they (Sadguru) have very nicely fulfilled the objectives of the government and aspirations of people. Farmers with small holdings have doubled or tripled their incomes due to Sadguru L. I. Schemes".

"Government officials also mentioned that unlike other NGOs who try to hog all the credit for themselves, Sadguru gives full credit to government and maintains good interpersonal relationship giving government personnel importance, respect and welcome".

"In its long relationship Sadguru has criticized and protested against government as well as given credit and unstinted praise to government whenever due. Sometimes Sadguru's criticism of government is in very harsh terms and pointedly at a particular office holder also".

"While it thus criticizes the government and sometimes severely, it also does not miss a single opportunity to give credit to government, appreciate its support and even praise it when problems are resolved."

"Sadguru's experience of partnering government has some important lessons both for GOs and NGOs".

"Sadguru's example shows that good performance is the best way to get

support from government. Inspite of all the self-righteous postures that NGOs tend to take, many of them fall woefully short of achieving results. If government is known for delays and in-competencies, NGOs record is not much better either. It was much easier for NGO- oriented government officers to support Sadguru even out of way, because Sadguru's performance in terms of quality, quantity and timeliness was excellent. Equally important is accounting and reporting. NGOs are generally known to be tardy if not down right defaulters in submitting their results, reports and accounts accurately and in time."

Donors — National and International

Since the inception of Sadguru, we have received funds from several non-Government funders and our relations with them all have been cordial and long lasting. From the information provided in Table 7.1, gives an idea of the types of major non-Government donors and the duration of our relationship with each of them.

Table 7.1: Types of Non-Government Donors and Duration of Sadguru's Relationship with Them

Sr. No.	Name of funding agency	Duration of relationship	Remarks
1.	Mafatlals - Standard Industries	24 years	They are still helping in raising corpus funds
2.	The Ford Foundation	11 years	
3.	Aga Khan Foundation	14 years	Including 8 year of EC funding through AKF
4.	NORAD, Royal Norwegian Embassy	13 years running	Ongoing - coming to an end due to gove-rnment policy
5.	Sir Dorabji Tata Trust	6 years running	Ongoing

6.	Sir Ratan Tata Trust	4th year running	Ongoing - committed up to 2005

The names of donors who have made only one-time grants / contributions to Sadguru for its corpus or a project do not appear in the table, as they are too many.

The Mafatlals - Standard Industries

The Mafatlals have been the first and foremost funder among the non-Government funding agencies. In fact they were the sponsorers of our activities as early as 1974. With nominal funds in the beginning for managerial expenses, they provided between Rs. 5-10 lakh every year till the year 1997. Though the amount was not big, it was of great significance in the beginning when managerial expenses were not available from other sources. Such support for a quarter of the century was very crucial for the organization for its existence and sustainability. Even in very difficult days for the textile industries, the Mafatlals continued their help. Some members of the Board of the Company told the Chairman, Shri Rasesh Mafatlal, to stop giving funds to Sadguru under the given circumstances. Shri Rasesh Mafatlal and some of his colleagues took a stand that when company was losing heavily, what difference it would make if it incurs a further loss of Rs 5-7 lakh a year.

More often than not in India when business houses support development programmes, they have some personal interest in the project area. The area could be an ancestral land, or it could be around their manufacturing units, or it could be an area from where they may be getting raw materials, or it may be an existing or potential market centre. None of these criteria applied to Mafatlals in any of their rural development projects. Very few business houses like Tatas, Mafatlals and few others have supported rural development projects without any business interests or emotional relations with the project area.

The Ford Foundation

The Ford Foundation was the first foreign funding agency to have given a grant to Sadguru Foundation. Two important aspects are worth mentioning in this context. The support from The Ford Foundation grant virtually initiated the process of funding from other sources that followed after the spread of word about the success of our irrigation cooperatives. It is not only that The Ford Foundation was the first foreign funding agency and it was also instrumental in getting us funds from the Aga Khan Foundation. It was The Ford Foundation and its then Programme Officer-Irrigation, Mr. Anthony Bottrall, who offered us the foreign fund for the first time and put us on international funding track. This relationship continued for more than 10 years.

Our experience in dealing with The Ford Foundation was pleasant. Their procedures were easy to understand and follow and were NGO friendly. As it was also our first experience with an International donor, we learnt a lot from The Ford Foundation and geared up ourselves to get into long term relationships with international organizations. What is of more important is that our capacity increased manifolds on account of The Ford Foundation's support and we became visible at the international level due to this support.

The Aga Khan Foundation (AKF)

Simultaneously with The Ford Foundation, the Aga Khan Foundation also became our funding partner from 1988 onward. This partnership went from strength to strength in terms of quantum of funds and also in relationship, till it came to an end in December 2001 after 14 years of long and extremely fruitful relationship. It first started with a small grant for meeting managerial expenses and from 1990 onwards, the programme funds also started coming in with a quantum rise from 1994 to 2001 under the European Union -assisted Community Managed Natural Resources (CMNR) project. The project was very successful as profusely appreciated by two international evaluations, Mid-Term and Final - done by international evaluators of the European Union.

It was during this period that Sadguru Foundation achieved the scaling up of its activities in NRM at the level, which is unmatched in the NGO sector. During that period, Sadguru grew from a small organization to a huge organization, increasing manifolds its capability and areas of operations. Our physical and financial progress was three times than what was planned in this partnership.

Throughout the 14 years of our relationship with AKF, it was a wonderful experience, working together. AKF at that time was very strict and strong in its monitoring system. We responded equally well to their strict monitoring norms and complied with all their requirements well in time in every case and in every situation. Sadguru got its strength in documentation and to an extent in reporting due to the partnership with AKF.

NORAD - The Royal Norwegian Embassy

The partnership with NORAD started in the beginning of 1991 and has been continuing since then. It started with a relatively small amount of Rs. 30 lakh (Rupees 3 million) a year and stabilized at about Rs. ten million a year in subsequent years. It has been a wonderful partnership with NORAD officials, who have been extremely cordial, supportive and full of understanding. It has been a pleasure to work with Scandanvian people and a Scandanvian organization. We have had very cordial relationship with all the officials of NORAD. Right from the very beginning from pre-appraisal itself, NORAD officials have been very supportive and encouraging to us. One Mission member of NORAD team, Mr. Thor Larsen said in his visit in 1991 that he had not seen such successful NRM project anywhere.

NORAD's procedures, reporting formats, have been NGO friendly, with minimum requirements. It has full understanding of the problems of NGOs and willing to listen to them and resolve their problems in pragmatic manners without any procedural hassles. Unfortunately, at the time of writing this book, our relationship with NORAD will come to an end soon, due to policy changes, both, at the GoI as well as that of Norwegian Government. Will deal with this development elsewhere in this book.

Sir Dorabji Tata Trust

It was a great gesture on the part of Tara Sabavala of Sir Dorabji Tata Trust to visit our organization in March 1997 with a view to grant us funds without our submitting any proposal. They had heard about our organization and indicated that they would like to visit our organization. After her visit, the Trust invited our proposal for the support. They thus started their support from the year 1997-98 and the support is continuing since then. On successful completion of three years project support, the Trust renewed its support for another three years increasing the quantum of support sizably. It has been the first Indian Trust offering substantial support to Sadguru Foundation. It has pragmatic policies and simple procedures. We have found it very pleasant and easy to work with. Consistent with Tata culture and tradition, the Trust officials have been very cordial, supportive and full of understanding. It has been also first funding agency to give corpus funds, increasing the quantum recently.

Sir Ratan Tata Trust (SRTT)

SRTT is our new funding partner since 2001 and the relationship is new and fresh. They have been our largest Indian funder and as we understand, we are perhaps their largest grantee as of 2003 in Rural Development. Before the approval of grants to our organization, the entire Board of Trustees of SRTT, under the Chairmanship of Ratan Tata, held a meeting with our organization at Mumbai. After the presentation of Sadguru's activities detailed interactions took place between the Board members of SRTT and Sadguru's representatives. Huge grant was approved after that.

Like AKF, SRTT also is very strict in monitoring and in various kinds of reporting requirements including yearly review of the programme by their review missions.

SRTT has also given us an endowment grant for our corpus fund worth Rs. one crore (Rs. 10 million) the biggest contribution made by any organization at that Point of time. It was conditioned to challenge fund of equal amount to be raised by Sadguru

Foundation in three years. We fulfilled this condition. It was a very business like condition in favour of NGO itself which helped us raise good endowment amount.

Our relationship with SRTT is relatively new and we are hopeful of a long and sustained relationship with them too, as we have always built long term relationship with all funding organizations.

Consultants

It is possible that international organizations working in India started using the services of consultants on regular basis as they had no time and manpower to do their work.

With our long existence and association with various funding organizations, national and international, we have come across and interacted with several consultants and several kinds of consultants. From raw and relatively inexperienced to highly seasoned and experienced consultants. For us it has been a mixed bag of experiences working with consultants. Sometimes we found their experience inadequate — being trained in an urban setting they were unable to relate to rural requirements — other times we found their knowledge lopsided and limited.

I believe that there should be a criteria for selection of consultants for evaluation. Some reliable information about their behaviour pattern should be collected before hand or the funding agency should brief the consultants about what is expected of them when they are on an evaluation mission of any organization. I believe, the qualifications, experience of the consultants should match with that of the standing and reputation of NGO to be evaluated. On the other hand there were people like Derek Poate who was sent by Aga Khan Foundation to advise and design our monitoring system. He developed a monitoring system on our existing system without adding or making drastic changes. He said, the organization should build up a monitoring system based on its own experiences and the system with which the organization is comfortable with. Consultant should offer simple and feasible suggestions.

Villagers

All the partnership of Sadguru and all our partners are of great importance and great value to us. These partnerships have helped in the growth and development of Sadguru in immeasurable terms. But of all the partnerships, the partnership with the villagers has been of the paramount importance. Our commitments are for the villagers. We work with them and for them. Our very existence is for the villagers. Without villagers and without their confidence in us, we have no reason to exist as an NGO.

Many people and institutions have studied various aspects of Sadguru. They have studied our village institutions, their functioning and their sustainability. But to my knowledge, hardly anyone has studied our relationship with the villagers. It is hardly documented. I don't know why researchers, evaluators, donors and many others, who were interested in various studies of Sadguru, never thought of studying Sadguru's relationship with the villagers. For their own reasons or for no reason, each of them have ignored or connived at this crucial aspect of Sadguru's relationship with the villagers.

As for me, I have cherished my intimate relationship with the villagers. I know that my physical contact with the villagers has reduced over time because of my increasing involvement in management and administrative responsibilities of Sadguru, emotionally I still continue to be greatly attached with the villagers. Of all the various groups and individuals that I have come across in my functioning, I relish most my interactions with the villagers. My villagers have their permanent place in my heart, not replaceable by any other group or people.

In my early days in this project, I had worked very closely with the villagers and the tribal people. I was in the field with the villagers from dawn to dusk. For the first few years, I was involved in everything that was happening in the villages under our programme. I was involved in the survey of lift irrigation sites, I was involved in the supervision of construction of lift irrigation schemes, constantly and regularly every day, I was involved in the operation of our first lift irrigation schemes. I was present almost whole night after night when irrigation was going on in the field under a lift irrigation scheme due to the electricity being available only at night. I was involved intensively in the beginning of all our new programmes such as check dams, forestry, and micro watershed, In the process, not only I developed good knowledge of the programme, but also cultivated relationship with the villagers.

The initial years of our organization were not 'happy-go-lucky days'. They were full of teething troubles and testing times. With all the troubles and turmoil that we faced in our initial years, what we pleasantly remember is the love showered on us by the local tribals after the initial testing period and teething problems had been overcome. I cherish their tremendous love, affection and support. We remember late Nurjibhai Damor, a leader from our oldest project village, Shankerpura, who would never tolerate any criticism of Sadguru by any one, telling people that criticizing Sadguru, would amount to committing a sin. Such deep sentimental respect for Sadguru not only helped in our survival, but served as much needed "tonic' for our growth.

In support of our initial sentimental relations with the villagers, I would like to reproduce a story from our Annual Report of the year ending 31st March 2002.

Box 7.4 - Lasting Sentimental Relations

Village Shankerpura was the first village chosen by Sadguru for its interventions, where a socio-economic survey was carried out in 1974-75 and the programme intervention in the form of first community lift irrigation started in the year 1976. Being the first major scheme in the entire region to have been set up by an NGOs or the Government, it was like a pilot project. The directors of the organization spent great deal of time and efforts in that village in the initial years. So intensive were the interactions that the directors had close personal relation with each and every household (about 150 at that time) and they knew everyone by first name.

At that time there were two main leaders in the village, Hirjibhai

Damor and Nurjibhai Damor, both cousin brothers. The local tribals have very sentimental tradition of sending green cobs of maize to their married daughters and sisters and after the daughters and sisters had tasted the first lot of maize cobs, the parents or head of the household would taste the maize cobs which are the staple food of local tribals. This tradition is being followed by all the tribal families in this region without any break. From the first year of the organization's association, Hirjibhai and Nurjibhai would first deliver the maize cobs to the Director's house and then they would start eating the new crops of maize cobs.

This is done every year since 1976. Nurjibhai died nearly 10 years ago and after that Hirjibhai alone continued the tradition of giving maize cobs to the Directors till today. Hirjibhai has reached the age of 75 years and not in good health and yet he has been carrying on the tradition. It is a very touching and sentimental relationship going on for 28 years between the NGO and a tribal village leader.

P.S. : When Hirjibhai visited my house in September 2003 to continue his tradition of offering maize cobs, I told him not to come due to his age and ill-health. He said, he would continue till he can travel in a bus. This was very touching moment. Hirji Bhai died in December 2004 and now this oldest village leader would never be visiting my house with fresh maize cobs.

There have been many such relationship with the villages and village leaders. Since the villages and village leaders are directly dealing with their village institutions, there is not much interactions at my level with the villagers in recent years. But, my colleagues in various departments dealing with different village institutions have similar intensive relationship with the village institutions and the villagers.

As I said in the beginning of this topic, the villagers are our most important partners. They have faith in our activities and integrity. There have been several examples when the politicians, like local MLAs and MPs had some problems with us on some occasion, the villagers stood strongly with us and as a result, the political leaders had to change their attitude towards us. Once when a local MP opposed some schemes, the villagers approached the

MP and made him to make a telephone call to the district officers showing his approval. Poisoned by the vested interest like the contractors and lower level staff of Irrigation Department, another MLA vehemently opposed any work entrusted to our organization in his constituency. Village leaders one after another met that MLA and convinced him about his wrong stance. Realizing the fact the MLA changed his attitudes and now he himself has approached Sadguru to get various schemes implemented.

Often we have come across incidences even in a state like Rajasthan where the villagers preferred to wait for our involvement rather than agreeing to have the scheme implemented by the Government department.

Good, sincere and fool proof work has won us the confidence of the villagers. Once, in Rajasthan, on the completion day of work on a check dam, all the villagers celebrated the occasion like a festival. Each family brought a coconut, Rs. 11/- each to be present to our masons and took them to the nearby bus station in a procession. This gesture was not only the appreciation of our work, but indicative of their confidence that this work is going to be useful to them for years.

A woman in Jhalawar, Rajasthan, after seeing water in her field, was so overjoyed that she said: what has happened in her village was not for her own generation alone, but, it was going to be useful to the future generation as the lives of their children have become secured. Therefore, just as we value the importance of our relationship with the villagers, the villagers in turn display great satisfaction and immense confidence in our association with them. Another incidence to support this statement is narrated below;

Box 7.5 - Sadguru's Work finds favour with the tribals

Once I was travelling by train. My fellow travellers were educated, local tribals, all serving in the Railways in good positions. Being local tribals, they knew our organization and its activities well. During the discussion, all of them said no other institution had done as much as Sadguru had done for the tribals in the district. They added that the contribution of their elected representatives (MLAs and MPs), though being tribal themselves, was not half of the contribution of Sadguru in the tribal region of the district. Once I happened to meet a senior government officer in Gujarat, a tribal from the same district, he said, "You and your organization do not require any introduction. Even a child in the district knows Sadguru well." This is the image and respect that we command among the tribal villagers and this is to us our real achievement. Very few NGOs occupy such an important position among the masses in the tribal regions.

CHAPTER - 8

Lessons And Directions For Future

Sadguru has completed 30 years ©of its work. It has made reasonably good progress and has contributed significantly to improving the socio-economic well being of poor people, especially the tribals in its project areas in the three states of Gujarat, Madhya Pradesh and Rajasthan. However, I must say that there are still many perplexing problems, particularly in the poor tribal areas and other under-developed regions that need to be resolved on a high priority basis including livelihood insecurity, poverty, degradation of natural resources and environment and further marginalization of the rural poor.

Besides, economic and political environment in India and the world is also changing in the wake of introduction of economic and administrative reforms, characterized by privatization, deregulation and globalization. Such changes have profound implications for India's economy in general and its rural sector in particular. In view of all this, I thought it was a right time now for Sadguru to look back and analyze its experiences and distil lessons that might be useful to it as well as to other NGOs and perhaps to rural development professionals. It is also appropriate at this juncture to look forward, determine directions for future work and charter a course of action for the next ten years or so. I attempt to do so in this chapter.

Determinants of Success of Sadguru's programmes

Sadguru's NRM and other rural development programmes have been judged by scholars, donors, government officers and other NGOs as highly successful. It would be relevant to reproduce what some distinguished independent persons said on the occasion of the Silver Jubilee function of Sadguru Foundation held in January 1999. I quote below some of the statements made at the occasion:

"I know the difficult times that Sadguru and its pioneers had in the beginning. Everyone including me was skeptical about the success of Sadguru's programmes. But these people had a clear-cut vision and enough courage to pursue their mission and programmes. There were very few supporters in the beginning. All alone these people struggled in the beginning. With the remarkable success that Sadguru achieved, now everyone is very supportive…". "They have proved that development around the available local resources with the participation of people is the most effective way of helping the poor. Every where in the world, on every forum, people are concerned about water and land. Sadguru has proved that when these two resources are harnessed properly, they can achieve amazing results. They have presented a development style and model, which is based on local resources supported with an appropriate technology. There are very few highly successful stories in the development field. Sadguru's development story has been one of the most successful ones. A Government of India report says that in the recent years, the forest cover / tree cover has increased by 60,000 hectares all over the country. Out of this, Sadguru's efforts alone have contributed about 14,000 hectares, which is not an ordinary achievement by a single NGO. It's a great development that tribal farmers opting for vegetable and tomato crops have started earning as much as rupees one lakh each per annum. A development model that Sadguru has offered, if replicated in the tribal regions from here to Kala Handi in Orissa, not only the tribals, but, the entire country will be rich. This model will tomorrow spread in the tribal regions of India and day after tomorrow in the entire world."

(Excerpts from the Presidential address delivered by Prof. Y. K. Alagh on the occasion of Silver Jubilee Celebrations of Sadguru Foundation).

"Sadguru's development journey has not been always a pleasant one. I was DDO in the District in 1981 and I saw their struggle. But, they have now created history in the rural and tribal development field. Sadguru is a model for the NGOs and even for the Government Departments. I would like such an effective NGO to extend their work in other Talukas and other Districts of the State. The Government will give all the necessary support. I am sure in another 25 years Sadguru will do still better work." -

Narayan Modi, IAS,
Former Commissioner and Secretary,
Tribal Development, Government of Gujarat.

"Sadguru has done marvelous work in its 25 years existence. I am a witness

of it. Because of its low profile and no publicity approach, the outside world is not aware of what Sadguru has achieved. It has achieved much more than many of the highly publicised development work elsewhere. People from everywhere should be brought to see what has been done here. At least the Gujarat Government should arrange visits of tribal and rural people to this project regularly, as visit to this work would provide tremendous motivation to the people. I wish their work and achievements are recognised and rewarded at the national and international levels."

Anil Shah, IAS (Retd.)
Former Secretary,
Rural Development, Government of Gujarat.

"The Institutions like Sadguru Foundation committed to prosperity, betterment and welfare of rural poor communities in the remote areas are the pride of nation".

Ms. Ela Bhatt,
Chairman, SEWA, Ahmedabad.

"The achievements of SWDF will certainly rank among the best endeavours of NGOs in the country and perhaps in the world. The achievements are particularly spectacular when we consider the fact that the organisation has been able to merge quality along with quantity - something that eludes so many other NGOs. What SWDF has to contribute is not merely in terms of direct benefits to the tribal population of Panchmahal and surrounding districts but also in terms of an approach to community service that other development agencies will do well to adopt."

E. M. Shashidharan,
Executive Director,
Development Support Centre, Ahmedabad.

"His (Jagawat's) work is very much in evidence as you drive through the rocky hills of Panchmahal in Gujarat. Lush green farms, soothing oasis in the dry, brown terrain now dot much of the district, a backward area of Gujarat. They are symbols of the dramatic transformation that Harnath Jagawat, 58, a former Personnel Officer in a Private Company, has brought in one of the country's most arid regions."

India Today of 15.01.1996

"The remarkable example that you have set for all of us in the development sector about what commitment for the poor, hard work, perseverance and single-

minded dedication to an organisation's goal can achieve. I hope that your dreams of Sadguru and its Training Centre becoming a resource centre for the spread of similar development across the tribal heart of India becomes a reality and that Government and other donors see the potentially critical role that Sadguru can play in this regard. I am sure that with concerted efforts from your side at Gnadhinagar, Jaipur, Bhopal and Delhi, a strong beginning can be made on this count."

Shanker Narayan,
Programme Officer,
AKF (Presently in The World Bank, New Delhi).

CONTRIBUTING FACTORS

The major contributing factors for the success of Sadguru's rural / tribal development programmes in Western Indian states are broadly as follows ;

- Selection of programmes based on available local natural resources and people's needs and priorities;
- Peoples involvement and participation in the programmes in cluding the management of the programmes;
- Considerable financial and other support from the Government and Non Government sources;
- Effective collaboration between the Government and Sadguru;
- Capability and expertise of Sadguru staff to formulate and implement the programmes successfully; and
- Professionalism in management and administration.

New Development Initiatives

In the next decade or so, Sadguru envisages to take up the following development initiatives:

- Replication of the Sadguru model of rural development with main focus on ;

(i) appropriate technologies for water resources development, conservation, use and management;

(ii) conservation, protection and optimum utilization of forest resources;

(iii) promotion of sustainable land use patterns through participatory watershed management approach and wastelands development through afforestation; and

(iv) building and empowerment of people's organizations.

- Agriculture and horticulture development through popularization of improved practices and provision of requisite in puts and services;
- Facilitating the value addition to agricultural, horticultural and forest produce through processing;
- Facilitating the marketing of agricultural produce at fair price;
- Conservation of bio-diversity through integrated pest and nutrition management;
- Diversification of income generating activities in both the ag ricultural sector and non-agricultural sector;
- Expansion of off-farm income generating activities associated with rural development;
- Public advocacy and networking with GOs and NGOs engaged in NRM and building their capacity through training and consultation;
- Upgrading the status of Sadguru Training Institute and launching of Management Development Programmes (MDPs) for middle level and senior NRM professionals in collaboration of the Institute of Rural Management, Anand (IRMA);
- Designing and launching a short term diploma course in NRM and in relevant subject in collaboration of the Institute of Rural Management, Anand (IRMA);

- Strengthening of Sadguru's in-house applied research and documentation facilities;
- Providing consultancy services in NRM to GOs and NGOs; and
- Mobilising funds for attaining financial self-sufficiency and institutionalisation of linkages with international, national andregional research, consultative, and other development estab lishments.

Replication of Sadguru Model

As I stated elsewhere in this book, the Sadguru model has community-based natural resources management at its core and water is used as an entry point. Sadguru with its vast and successful experience of 30 years in the field of natural resources and rural development plans to share its experience and the lessons learnt with GOs and NGOs engaged in rural development in India and other developing countries of the world. This is based on our conviction built over the last 30 years that the model has great relevance and potential for replication in regions having agro-climatic and socio-economic conditions comparable to those in Sadguru's project areas.

These models which have evolved around degraded natural resources that have the potential to make life worth living, whether it is in India, south Asia or Central and Western Africa. Sadguru's experience could be pertinent in the fields of natural resources management and integrated rural development. I believe Sadguru has a job carved out for it for the next quarter of the century and even beyond. The NRM technologies that are evolved and successfully replicated, the social management of resource systems and the professional approach towards human development are the key elements that need to be replicated on a large-scale expansion first in western India and then in other parts of the country and elsewhere. Currently, Sadguru is focusing on the other tribal states of India where the problems are acute and the conditions are similar. Besides, concurrently, we are also engaged in expanding our horizons to similar regions and areas in developing countries, especially in central and east African countries.

Potential for Replication

Sadguru's model of water-centered development with focus on natural resources management has great potential in India and also in other similar regions in India inhabiting about 90 million people, mostly tribals, and abroad. The Government, International Organizations and NGOs have to rise to the occasion to translate this enormous potential into concrete benefits to the poor people living in those fragile areas.

The leaders and people have been talking of second green revolution in our country, not knowing how and from where it would come. I strongly feel that such second green revolution will come from the existing vulnerable and backward districts mostly from the tribal regions as such regions have potential to develop their agriculture and related activities manifolds.

Over the next 10 - 15 years, Sadguru would play an important role directly through replicating the programme in other areas and indirectly through supporting other agencies, both GOs and NGOs, by way of building their capacity through exposure visits to Sadguru's projects and training at its Training Institute in Chosala. Several visitors from African countries have found Sadguru model very much relevant and replicable in their regions.

More than 70 % of the total tribal population of our country is concentrated in eight States, namely Bihar, Jharkhand, Orissa, Madhya Pradesh, Chhattisgarh, Gujarat, Rajasthan and Maharashtra. The tribal belt runs across the country from east to West and forms an almost contiguous region having many similarities.

By any yardstick or indicator the tribal regions of these eight States are among the most backward and poor. Yet, to repeat, paradoxically, all these regions are rich in natural resources of land, water and forests, and therefore, these regions and their people ought not to have been so poor. I am not going to deal with the mineral resources of these regions. Its a different story by itself. But it is a pity that the mining and industrial development based on such minerals have not helped the local tribals. This incidentally is a pointer to those who think the industrial development as solution for the removal of tribal poverty.

Now, I briefly describe the nature of the NRM problems and how they were addressed by Sadguru and how Sadguru's experience could be replicated in similar areas elsewhere in India and Abroad.

Water Resources Development and Management

Water is essential for survival of all living beings on this planet earth and is a catalyst of development. Sadguru considered it as the focal point in its natural resource development projects. The natural cycle begins with water and ends with water. The crisis of fresh water that India and many other developing countries are currently facing is alarming. This is due mainly to the ever increasing human and animal population and the associated activities and the wasteful use of available water resources. In thousands of villages in India, even drinking water is not available throughout the year. Unless fresh water is conserved and judiciously used for meeting various consumptive and productive requirements, the crisis will remain inescapable. Development of new water resources is one of the biggest challenges that India is facing now. Ensuring equitable distribution of available water and access of millions of the poor to it are other burning issues. The fugitive (mobile) nature of water creates further complexities in its exploitation and judicious use. Often the marginalized segments of the society, especially the poor tribals, suffer the most due to the scarcity of water. The rich and the powerful have had access to water for centuries and have exploited the resource using technologies suitable for plains areas. As a result, the disparity in the distribution of water between the rich and the poor in society has further increased.

For addressing these problems, it is necessary to evolve cost-effective technologies suitable for uplands and marginal lands, invest in replicating these technologies, and make water accessible to the poor. Sadguru has demonstrated that it is possible by creating small-scale decentralized water resource systems that can reach the poor so that they get what rightfully is theirs. The surface and ground water development and management systems developed and used extensively by Sadguru have the potential for expansion within its existing project areas and elsewhere in the nearby and far away areas in other states in India having similar agro-climatic and socio-cultural environment. Besides, the model developed and refined over the last 30 years has immense scope for replication in many developing countries also. Sadguru would take this up as a major challenge and strive to replicate the model through expansion, consultation, exposure visits, exchange of information, and field training. The need for developing human resources to meet this challenge would also be addressed.

Check dams

In these eight tribal-dominated States, where more than 70 % of nation's tribal population resides, the average annual rainfall is about 1000 mm, and the range is 800 mm to 1,600 mm. The topography of most of these tribal areas is undulating and the landscape is crisscrossed by intensive network of rivers, rivulets, and nallas. There is enormous scope for surface water harvesting in the region through small masonry structures, small check dams and small bandharas, which are more suitable to the tribal areas and more beneficial to the local tribal people. According to my rough estimates, there is a scope for constructing more than 50,000 small check dams in the tribal regions of these eight States. This assumption is based on our first hand knowledge of eight tribal districts in three states that we have been working. By check dam I mean those which store tangible water. Each of my estimated check dam with tangible storage would benefit minimum of 50 families and at an average more than 100 families. This programme alone may benefit about 30 million of tribal population of above states.

Lift irrigation

For the rural people which also includes the tribal people, no programme is better than the provision for irrigation. Ask any tribal farmer as to what is his most felt need and the spontaneous and invariably the answer will be "irrigation water". It is also an accepted fact now that for the tribal regions, lift irrigation is the most appropriate method for irrigation as the flow irrigation / gravity irrigation is by and large not feasible under the conditions prevailing in the tribal regions, including undulating topography. Sadguru experience in the tribal districts of Gujarat, Rajasthan and Madhya Pradesh has demonstrated not only the potential for lift irrigation, but, also the capability of the tribals to manage those community lift irrigation projects successfully.

On a rough estimate, there is scope for about 20,000 community lift irrigation projects in the tribal regions of the eight States mentioned above. This estimate is based on our experiences as well as detailed technical study of eight tribal districts in the Western regions. Even at an average of 100 acres per such L. I. Scheme, the irrigation can be created for minimum of ten lakhs acres. This is of community lift irrigation schemes and not of a small group or individual lift irrigation through portable pumps of 5-10 HP. Technically, a scheme installed with 5-10 HP is also lift irrigation. But, it is an individual L. I. Scheme or at the most of a group of few farmers. These are certainly not the community lift irrigation schemes. If we consider the potential of such individual or group L. I. Schemes, there could be potential for more than 40,000 such L. I. Schemes.

There are other equally important programmes like intensive micro watershed development, and farm forestry, which have great potential in the tribal areas, and when they are integrated with the water resources development, benefits from them could be unbelievably high. However, the potentials of watershed development and forestry are also so immense that they need to be dealt with elaborately and separately, which I cannot do in this brief presentation.

Coming back to the potentials of the water resources development in the tribal regions, what is required to be done to translate this potential into concrete action and actual benefits is, in the first instance, a strong political will. The State and Central Governments have to be serious towards these potentials. It is high time that the policy makers gave due priorities to the development of local resources through small projects. It is a pity that for some reasons only mega projects attract the attention of policy makers and implementers. The mega projects make big news. A small project, howsoever beneficial it may be, does not attract the attention of anyone. It does not make any news. But, many such small projects put together make them equal to a mega project, besides the advantages of better viability and easier manageability.

We have now started planning for interlinking India's rivers so that water from surplus areas could be brought to water scarce parts of our country. This is necessary in our country. But it would be a criminal negligence on the part of policy makers and planners if they continue to deprive the poor tribals of the benefits from their local natural resources. I can quote a number of examples in which the Government have spent hundreds of crores of rupees on irrigation projects, constructed in the tribal areas, but, most of the benefits of those projects have gone to the developed areas elsewhere and to relatively rich people. What hurts me more is, however, not the benefits going to other better off people, but the Government's apathy towards the needs of poor local tribals and its failure to allocate small amount of funds, say even five to ten crore rupees per year, for development of small projects in the tribal districts. This policy is not fair and is simply anti-poor, and therefore, it has to be discontinued forthwith. I would argue that, along with mega projects, small / minor irrigation projects also should receive equal importance in terms of allocation of resources.

In our country, unfortunately, the Government often responds to the pressure tactics. Without pressure, hardly anything happens, even for the most genuine cause. It is time that tribal leaders and tribal people formed a strong lobby and applies pressure on the policy makers for the realization of the development potentials in the tribal regions.

The tribals have been denied the fruits of development and

have been denied the access to their own local resources for too long a period. This has to be reversed at the earliest, otherwise it would be too late. Just as the justice delayed is justice denied, similarly the development delayed is development denied. The tribals should no longer be denied the benefits of development through neglect and delays.

However, it must be mentioned that recently many of the State Governments have started giving importance to the small scale water resources projects, particularly, check dams. Some states have taken up massive programme of small scale water harvesting structures-check dams. This is good development. Unfortunately, in large number of such small scale water harvesting structures-check dams, the quality is not maintained, and as a result, the investment is wasted. Many such check dams constructed under watershed development programme and under different programmes have been washed away in first good monsoon. I strongly feel that if designs and workmanship of such check dams are up to mark, there is no question of their being washed away. The technology is full proof if technical components and parameters are fully met. Very interestingly, large numbers of check dams of high profile NGO have also been washed away in the monsoon of 2003. For this, the NGO blames the monsoon and the Government. Monsoon for good rains and the Government for allegedly releasing the water from upstream dam. Both these arguments are unacceptable and untenable. Masonry check dams of proper design and quality workmanship can never be washed away and should never be washed away due to excess of rains.

Very strangely, we have heard that in Gujarat the water resources department has changed the design of the check dams from masonry to cement concrete (cc) structures. The only reason offered for such shifting from masonry to cc could be the safety of structures. There are large numbers of examples when designs and workmanship of masonry structures have been up to the mark, nothing has happened to such structures. Why then shifting to higher cost cc structures ? Is it for the safety of the structures or safety of the engineers who have designed and executed such structures ? Even very small check dams on drainage line, where gabion structures or grade stabilizers could have served the purpose, the cc structures are created or proposed under the Panchayat Minor Irrigation works. If Gujarat Government or District Panchayat under their minor irrigation works have decided for cc check dams, it should be stopped forthwith as there is no justification for cc check dam.

Land Resources Development and Management

Enhancing and maintaining the productivity of land in the semi-arid tropics of India, which is a major source of livelihood for millions of poor people, is another great challenge. For centuries, this land fulfilled the needs of not only human but also every living being. These lands over the years have been over-exploited by the human race. Mahatma Gandhi once said that mother earth can fulfill the needs of every living being but not the greed of every individual. Over the years unplanned development and ever expanding population over-exploited the valuable resource. As a result the soils have become less productive and can no longer bear the burden of increasing human and animal population. As I said earlier, it is the poor, who often bears the consequences of such degradation whether they are party to it or not. They have learned to cope with such consequences and use a variety of coping mechanisms to maintain their subsistence level of living under such harsh conditions.

Sadguru has been engaged in rejuvenating these degraded lands through various technologies; one of them being integrated watershed development which is time tested and well researched over the years. We have observed that unless the watershed approach with the involvement of people is adopted to manage and utilize such lands, they cannot be made productive. The recent efforts made in India and elsewhere in the sub-continent to conserve these watersheds using the decentralized and bottom-up approach are the efforts in the desirable direction. The application of right methodology, which does not interfere with biological diversity of the environment, is what is needed for maximizing the productivity of land and other natural resources. Sadguru has already created a visible positive impact in the semi-arid tropics of western India through this approach. The impact has widely been acknowledged by international research institutions, practitioners and policy makers and planners world over. Particularly, the approach has been found to be relevant to the central and east African countries. Sadguru is willing to play a critical role in the replication of its technologies in these countries.

Sadguru has been successful in training and providing technical inputs to several GOs and NGO partners in the watershed technologies, building and managing people's institutions, and increasing agricultural and horticultural productivity in dry lands. Through such training and technical inputs, Sadguru has been indirectly instrumental in covering about two lakhs hectares of the land (about 5 lakhs acres of the land through such GOs and NGOs). This role will be intensified and extended further by way of training, consultation, exchange and dissemination of experience and public advocacy. Further expansion of the Sadguru approach in the neighbouring regions directly or indirectly would also be taken up. Sadguru has played an advisory role in several forums and consultative groups at the State and Central levels. This role will be further strengthened in the next decade when Sadguru plans to expand its horizons to support other states and other countries with similar complexities in dealing with poverty and natural resources-related problems.

Forest Resource Conservation and Management

Conservation of forest resources is the crying need of the day. While pursuing our economic interests, we have done so much damage to our natural resources and environment that our own survival is threatened. We all, whether poor or rich, depend on environment for our survival and well being. There is need for drastic change in the way we have treated our natural resources, especially our forest resources, in the second half of the 19th century and the whole of the 20th century. People who are part and parcel of the natural resource systems were kept out and often exploited and victimized in the process of development. Although all of our natural resources have been degraded, forests have suffered most. Their area, productivity and production have all been declining over time due to growing biotic and biotic pressures and flawed policies and programmes of the government. In the past, forests had been viewed by the State as the major source of easy liquidity. This resulted in their depletion and degradation. Besides, their tangible and intangible benefits were grossly under-valued and their real value was not reflected in India's gross domestic product (GDP). Consequently, allocation to the forestry sector was also not commensurate with its real contribution to the economy. It is high time now that we reversed these trends and restore, conserve and enhance our forest resources in the interest of millions of the poor who depend on them for their survival. And at the same time we must also conserve and enhance the biological diversity.

Sadguru over the years has established ways and means of conserving the wealth of forests in semi-arid tropical lands with people's involvement. Creating alternative sources such that people no longer need to depend solely on forest is one of the most viable options. In developing countries, most of the rural poor people largely depend on forests for their livelihood and meet their basic requirements for fodder, fuel and other non-timber forest produce from forests. Timber needs even if existing are basically domestic and not commercial. The best way to reduce pressure on forests and at the same time achieve self-sufficiency in domestic requirement is by promoting agro-forestry and other similar practices. These interventions have the potential to regenerate a new social and ecological cycle that is self-sustaining in itself. The importance of agro forestry could be understood well with the example of district Anand in Gujarat which does not have any forest land, and yet, it has the largest number of trees in the state under agro forestry plantation.

It has been our experience at Sadguru that the above-mentioned approaches have elevated women's status in society, reduced their drudgery, enhanced their financial capacity to cope with contingencies at household level, and restored the degraded natural forests. They need to be replicated elsewhere in India and other countries. The lessons learnt over the years need to be shared, and put into action in new areas. The solutions that Sadguru has found out have the potential for wider adoption. There is need for publicity, exchange of experiences, public advocacy and mutual consultation to do this. Sadguru in the next decade is willing to shoulder the responsibility to share, exchange and replicate its approaches in natural resources development and management in India and abroad. As we have observed in the case of Ethiopia, there is need for replication of Sadguru's JFM models under their Area Enclosure projects. Besides, Sadguru's work in small-scale water resources development and micro watershed development also offer opportunities for wider replication. Similar is the case with many other developing countries.

Apart from the above mentioned challenges, there is also need to address several emerging second-generation issues in coming years. Such issues include the need for value addition to farm produce to meet the new demands, better marketing facilities, and enhanced access to common resources and facilities. Both Sadguru and people in its project areas are aware of these second-generation problems.

For this Sadguru needs to work on the policy and research front. Mobilizing opinion makers, creating public awareness, formation of village institutions and creating a conducive environment to promote sustainable people-centered natural resource management strategy will be on its agenda in the future.

Community Empowerment and Participation

Growth with justice should be the sole motto of any intervention aimed at ensuring that the benefits reach the poorest. Quite often the social development approaches and resource conservation measures end up benefiting the already well-off segments of the society. They seldom reach the poor or the disadvantaged. The "actors" have to consciously make attempts to target their initiatives precisely at the poor and continuously advocate for the rights of 'disadvantaged' over common pool natural resources. Sadguru believes in social justice, gender equity and rights of future generations over the natural resource systems and has created models, which have been instrumental in bringing about the complete transformation of tribal areas, benefiting several hundreds of thousands of families.

But, still, there are thousands of such villages on the periphery of Sadguru's project areas, which are eagerly awaiting the redressal of their miseries. Sadguru will attempt to reach out to those areas with feasible approaches built around community-based integrated NRM interventions. This will improve the economic condition of people and restore the degraded environment. Anticipating sustainable growth in agricultural productivity, Sadguru will also address issues of appropriate marketing, processing infrastructure, which is necessary for value addition to the agricultural produce. Besides, Sadguru also envisages for itself an active role in mobilizing the resources necessary for creating the above-mentioned infrastructure and facilities and will make sure people have access to them. Apart from this, Sadguru will also be instrumental in encouraging diversified and widespread agricultural growth. This is sought to be achieved through establishment of new village institutions, further strengthening of the existing village institutions, and preparing them to face the new challenges. This will make the existing partnership stronger.

To conclude this section, I would like recapitulate for my readers what, in 1951, Mr. K.M. Munshi, the then Agriculture Minister, Government of India and a great planner, philosopher of India, stated in a seminar, which I reproduce: "Study the life's cycle in the villages under your charge in both its aspects - hydrological and nutritional. Find out whether the cycle has been disturbed and estimate the steps necessary for restoring it. Work out the village plan in four of its aspects: (i) existing conditions, (ii) steps necessary for completing the hydrological cycle, (iii) steps necessary to complete the nutritional cycle and a complete picture of the village when the cycle is restored, and (iv) have faith in your self and the programme. Nothing is too mean and nothing is too difficult for the man who believes that the restoration of the life's cycle is not only essential for freedom and happiness of India but is essential for her / his very existence".

Attaining Financial Self Reliance

Attaining and retaining financial self-sufficiency is a pre-requisite for survival, success, and growth of any organization including NGOs. Duly recognizing this, Sadguru has been trying to be financially self-reliant. This has become even more important now when many a good foreign donors are withdrawing their financial support to development programmes in India. I will briefly describe in this section Sadguru's efforts and struggle to mobilize funds for its programmes. Like its progress in physical activities, Sadguru's financial progress in the beginning of the organization was very modest and the sources of funds were also limited.

During the first phase spanning over 8 years,1974 to 1981, the total fund mobilization and utilization was of the order of Rs. 12.58 million, i.e., at an average Rs. 1.57 million per year. The major sources were the STANROSE Mafatlals for the managerial cost and the Government for the programme cost.

During the second phase of another 8 years (1982 to 1989), the expenditure was Rs. 68.40 million, i.e., at an average of Rs. 8.55 million per year. The increase in this phase was nearly six times the level achieved in the preceding 8 years. The major sources during this period were the Government, The Ford Foundation, Aga Khan Foundation and STANROSE Mafatlals.

During the third phase of 4 years (1990 to 1993), the expenditure was Rs. 138.46 million, i.e., at an average of Rs. 34.62 million per year. The expenditure in this period of 4 years was almost double that of the combined expenditure incurred in the first and second phases of 8 years each. The major sources were the Government, Aga Khan Foundation, The Ford Foundation, NORAD, STANROSE Group and Beneficiaries contribution in kind.

During the period of last ten years (1994 to March 2004), the mobilization and expenditure was about Rs. 917.17 million i.e. average Rs. 91.71 million per year.

The quantum increase in the availability of funds is reflected in the above analysis, which in turn reflects the popularity and the success of the programmes and credibility of Sadguru in delivering the goods.

Sadguru has been successful in mobilizing funds from multiple sources. The Government, states and central, international organizations, private trusts, etc. In any given year, about 15 agencies have been providing financial support to Sadguru.

The organization is also working to raise corpus funds in order to have sufficient cushioning and reasonable self-support for its establishment and management cost in the future. It has set a target of raising at least Rs. 15 crores for its corpus funds. I am happy to say that nearly 65 % of this set target has been achieved and we are hopeful that in near future the full target will be achieved. For long term sustainability of Sadguru as an organization, Sadguru has started building such corpus funds.

However, in view of the rapidly changing national and international economic and political environment, particularly the changing political situation in India, changes in priorities of international donor agencies, and likely changes in institutional leadership, I perceive a great deal of risk and uncertainty in raising enough funds to attain financial self-sufficiency.

However, I do feel confident that under any adverse circumstances, such as the external factors the set back could be temporary as any organization with good track record and reputation will find necessary support from some sources.

Consultancy, Networking And Public Advocacy

There are also few options through which Sadguru can achieve financial self-sufficiency. I perceive a lot of scope for Sadguru to provide consultancy services in the field of NRM to GOs and NGOs in both India and abroad. Already, quite a few NGOs and

GOs are availing our services, particularly training and expert advice in designing water harvesting structures and implementing watershed development projects. The offers have been constantly coming from various agencies to avail our services in providing inputs to various NGOs in strengthening their capacity. As we have expertise in water resources development and related fields, our entering into professional consultancies may ensure our financial security. Even industries are seeking our help in building water harvesting structures for their requirements. We are resisting this temptation as right now we don't want to deviate from own main mission to help rural communities. Also, the programmes of Sadguru are very much financially viable, and therefore, in the worst scenario, some programmes could be implemented through institutional finances from the banks, NABARD, etc.

Conservation of biological diversity and natural resources is the major crisis imposing greater threat to the nation's economy. The magnitude and complexity of these problems are so large that they could only be tackled by decentralized local and regional alternatives. Thus those who took over the responsibility to create sustainable environment, need to make some concrete efforts while addressing micro issues. Hence in this complex development context, collective action could only bring desired changes.

To evolve successful alternatives for the problems related to natural resources, considerable efforts are being made by the Government Departments, Funding Agencies and NGOs. Somehow these efforts remain isolated, therefore it is important to share and exchange ideas and complexities related to innovative resource management systems, professional approaches towards human development and technologies that are successfully replicated. Hence an Environment Conservation Forum was launched by Sadguru to provide a common platform to all the partners, viz., Government Departments, Funding Agencies, Academicians, Researchers, NGOs and Village Institutions to share their ideas.

Specifically, the Environment Conservation Forum (ECF) has the following objectives:

- to enhance the qualitative inputs of partners (partner organizations as well as village institutions) in their work on NRM;
- to muster better co-ordination among partners in forest resources, water resources;
- to improve micro-watershed treatment and to bring out regional issues in these sector;
- to increase visibility of the issues and concerns on national and international platform by undertaking policy advocacy, research, capacity building and networking among the regional partners; and
- to establish linkages with the academic and research Institutions, training institutions, practitioners, national and international organizations, to promote environmental interests of the region.

Presently Environment Conservation Forum is actively functioning in Gujarat, Rajasthan and Madhya Pradesh in the area of networking by coordinating and also representing regional issues. At an appropriate time, the scope may be expanded to other areas.

Over the 30 years, N. M. Sadguru Water and Development Foundation, popularly known as Sadguru, has successfully used Public Advocacy as an instrument of persuading the Government of Gujarat and Government of India to effect the pro-poor changes in their policies, particularly, in the field of water resource development and management. Sadguru's good success and public advocacy could be attributed to the fact that it is involved in doing the things and due to track record of doing things with success, its advocacy arguments on various issues are usually listened to and responded favourably by the Government. This role of Sadguru has been mentioned earlier in this book. We envisage that this role of public advocacy in NRM will be more effectively played by Sadguru by virtue of its long standing experiences and strong relationship with the bureaucracy and the government.

References & Bibliography

1. Chopra, K., G.K. Kadekodi and M.N. Murthy (1990) Participatory Development: An Approach to the management of Common Property Resources, Sage Publications, New Delhi.

2. Jagawat, Harnath (2000) Watershed Management: Last Chance for the Revival of Rural Ecology and Economy. Paper presented at a Workshop on Watershed Management organized by the Confederation of Indian Industries at Hotel Taj Mahal, New Delhi, on 2nd November 2000.

3. Jagawat, Harnath (2000) A Note submitted to the Planning Commission of Government of India on Watershed Development, Rainfed Farming and Natural Resources Management for Tenth Five Year Plan, December 2000.

4. Jagawat, Harnath (2002) Need to Provide Greater Scope to NGOs in National Development - A paper presented at a Conference on "Role of NGOs in National Development", organized by the Planning Commission, Government of India at Vigyan Bhavan, New Delhi, April 20, 2002.

5. Jagwat, Harnath (forthcoming) Watershed Development: An Opportunity for Corporate Sector. Book chapter in "A Diverse Test of Reality: Convergence and Synergy" Confederation of Indian Industries, New Delhi (forthcoming).

6. Jagawat, Harnath (2002) Natural Resources Management (NRM): A Solution to Tribal Poverty in India. A country paper presented at an ILO Regional Workshop at Chiang Mai, Thailand, December 2-5, 2002.

7. Jagawat, Harnath (2003) Role of Corporate Sector in Watershed Management. Keynote address delivered at a workshop on "Corporate Sector Role in Watershed Management", organized by the Confederation of Indian Industries at Hotel Oberoi, New Delhi, on February 7th, 2003.

8 Jagawat, Harnath (2003) Appropriate Technology Transfer in Natural Resource Management and Poverty Alleviation - An Experience of an NGO in Western India. A paper presented at the International Conference on Technology Transfer and Capacity Building, jointly organised by the Ministry of Environment, Norway and UN at Trondheim, Norway, June 23-27, 2003.

9. Jagawat, Harnath (2003) Revival of Rivers - An illustrative story of the revival of several rivers and rivulets through an appropriate and effective strategy in water harvesting in the tribal regions of Western India - updated in July 2003.

10. NIRD (2000) Rural Development Statistics, National Institute of Rural

Development, Hyderabad.

11. Parikh K. S. and R. Radhakrishnan (eds.) (2002) India Development Report, New Delhi : Oxford University Press.
12. Unfolding our future (1999) - Strategic Report, N M Sadguru Water and Development Foundation, Dahod.
13. Singh Katar (1994) Managing Common Pool Resources : Principals and Case Studies, Oxford University Press, Delhi.
14. Singh Katar (1995) "People's Participation in Managing Common Pool Resources", Social Change, 25(1).
15. Singh, Katar (1999) Rural Development : Principles, Policies and Management, Sage, New Delhi.
16. Singh, Katar and Gupta, K.K. (1997) The Sadguru Model of Community-Based Natural Resources Management.
17. WCED (1987) Our Common Future, World Commission on Environment and Development Stockholm.

Abbreviations

1.	AKF	Aga Khan Foundation
2.	CAG	Controller and Auditor General
3.	CC	Cement Concrete
4.	CCF	Chief Conservator of Forests
5.	CAPART	Council for Advancement of Peoples Action and Rural Technology
6.	CMNR	Community Managed Natural Resources
7.	DFO	District Forest Officer
8.	DPAP	Drought Prone Area Programme
9.	DRDA	District Rural Development Agency
10.	DSP	Deputy Superintendent of Police
11.	EC	European Commission
12.	ECF	Environment Conservation Forum
13.	FPCs	Forest Protection Committees
14.	GDP	Gross Domestic Product
15.	GOs	Government Organisations
16.	GoI	Government of India
17.	HP	Horse Power
18.	HRD	Human Resource Development
19.	IAS	Indian Administrative Service
20.	ILO	International Labour Organisation
21.	IRMA	Institute of Rural Management, Anand
22.	JFM	Joint Forest Management
23.	JRY	Jawahar Rozgar Yojana
24.	LAMPS	Large Area Multi Purpose Cooperative Societies
25.	LI	Lift Irrigation
26.	LIC	Lift Irrigation Cooperative
27.	LIS	Lift Irrigation Scheme
28.	MCFT	Million Cubic Feet
29.	MDPs	Management Development Programmes
30.	MLAs	Members of Legislative Assembly
31.	MP	Madhya Pradesh

32.	MPs	Members of Parliament
33.	NABARD	National Bank for Agriculture and Rural Development
34.	NGOs	Non Government Organisations
35.	NIRD	National Institute of Rural Development
36.	NORAD	Royal Norwegian Embassy
37.	NRM	Natural Resources Management
38.	PCCF	Principal Chief Conservator of Forests
39.	PISs	Project Implementation Agency
40.	PRIs	Panchayati Raj Institutions
41.	NMSWDF	N M Sadguru Water and Development Foundation
42.	SC	Scheduled Caste
43.	SE	Superintending Engineer
44.	SEWA	Self Employed Women's Association
45.	SHGs	Self Help Groups
46.	SRTT	Sri Ratan Tata Trust
47.	ST	Scheduled Tribes
48.	SSSST	Shri Sadguru Seva Sangh Trust
49.	WC	Watershed Committee

Afterword

The man behind the mission

Harnath Jagawat, the agent of change, was inspired to step in this field as a result of his constructive experiences in his village in Ekkalgarh.

He says:

My ancestral village Ekkalgarh is a very small village. The total number of households in the village is still less than 100. It retains its typical rustic appearance, beauty and culture. The two rivers, Chambal and Kshipra, keep it fertile. Its numerous nallas (streams) provide water for at least eight months in a year. A sizeable proportion of its land is grassland, which produces sufficient quantity of forage grasses to meet the requirement of village animals. Though there is no forestland in the village, its extensive tree cover provides enough fuel wood and timber to meet the requirements of the village.

Two aspects of the village have always attracted me — its loving people and the river Chambal. Both have a special place in my life. Till the age of 35, I stayed mainly in Vadodara, where I was educated and also served for about 10 years as an executive in the corporate sector company. Though Vadodara, is a very beautiful city, but my fascination for my village was much more. Every summer and Diwali vacation, I caught the first available train and went to my village. I used to spend about three months every year in the village. Most of my time during such a vacation was spent swimming and playing in river Chambal with friends and cousins.

Development: Bane or Boon

Chambal was among the cleanest rivers in India. One could use its water as a mirror. Sadly industrial development has lead to Chambal's pollution, particularly, after Kota. The portion of river near my village is still very clean, except, occasionally when its waters get polluted with what local people call "Birla Water" (Birla ka pani). A plant owned by the Birla's Gwalior Rayon Company (GRASIM) situated at Nagda on the bank of river Chambal discharges a huge quantity of effluents into the water periodically. The river remains polluted for a few days. During one of my visits to the village recently, I saw this red water. I was shocked. Can Birlas' being such a big influential industrial house in India be punished for polluting?

It is sad that, in India, politically and financially powerful people are rarely punished for such crimes. An occasional Supreme Court intervention creates some ripples, ultimately, everything settles down and things remain unchanged. In Western or Northern countries, the governments win or lose elections on pollution and environmental issues. In this country, perhaps polluting agencies are so powerful that they can think of de-stabilizing the government and in most cases afford to flout the environmental laws. Every time any industry(s) is given notice for closure for polluting, it defends itself on grounds of employment and our trade unions also support it. Everyone tends to ignore that for every 1,000 people employed by such industries, more than five times people are affected by the polluting industry. Our industries, metropolises, urban centres are converting our rivers into gutter systems. And we remain helpless spectators.

My interest, my future

My village background and intensive training and exposure in the field of rural development during my post-graduation studies at the MS University of Baroda, motivated me to serve rural people. However, such an opportunity came very late in my life — there were very few NGOs working in the field and, therefore, few opportunities for trained social workers. There were a few Gandhian NGOs, but most of them were not keen to employ qualified professionals.

In between, in a curious turn of event, the Mafatlals group was divided in three separate sub-groups in 1978 and so were their rural development projects. Each company was assigned different rural development projects. Our project in Dahod was assigned to the Standard Mills, and therefore, it went to Rashesh Mafatlal, the youngest of three Mafatlal brothers.

After the above division, we continued working under the banner of SSST, which eventually went to Arvind Mafatlal. Due to legal and administrative problems, a separate organization in the name of Navinchandra Mafatlal Sadguru Water and Development Foundation was established and since early 1986 we have been working under this new name but with the same management at the project level. In the beginning for about four years, united Mafatlal Group supported our activities in Dahod and thereafter from 1978 the Standard Industries headed by Rashesh Mafatlal supported the project. The support continued till 1997-98. Though the money provided was a small when compared to our budget, particularly in the last few years, it was crucial for the survival and growth of the organisation. The managerial expenses for several years were met from the contribution of support of the Mafatlals. This provided a great deal of security to the organization and paved a way for further progress through funds from various other sources. My wife and I were on the pay-roll of Mafatlal Company and this arrangement continued up to the year 2000.

In the last 12 years, Sadguru has expanded its activities manifolds. Rashesh Mafatlal as Chairman of our Board has supported us throughout. Sadguru and Harnath Jagawat continue their mission unflaggingly.